THE

Christmas Fire-Side;

OR, THE

JUVENILE CRITICS.

BY

SARAH WHEATLEY,

AUTHOR OF "THE FRIENDLY ADVISER."

LONDON

PRINTED FOR LONGMAN, HURST, REES, AND ORME,
PATERNOSTER-ROW; AND J. HARRIS, CORNER
OF ST. PAUL'S CHURCH-YARD.

1806.

Printing Statement:

Due to the very old age and scarcity of this book,
many of the pages may be hard to read due to the
blurring of the original text, possible missing pages,
missing text, dark backgrounds and other issues
beyond our control.

Because this is such an important and rare work, we
believe it is best to reproduce this book regardless of
its original condition.

Thank you for your understanding.

CONTENTS.

A 3

PREFACE.

VIRTUE, the more intimately she is known, will be the more admired; and to trace her actions to their source may lead us, in the end, to emulate them. "It is impossible," says an elegant adage, "to pass through the aromatic groves of Arabia, without bearing away some of their sweets and fragrance." Example has always been said to make a deeper impression on the mind than precept; and to search into the motives and merits of those celebrated actions, which are held out as examples, and compare their relative excellence, may serve to fix the impression still deeper. Young people,

therefore, cannot too soon be taught to
make such examinations and comparisons:
for, while it must necessarily tend to
strengthen and confirm their moral principles, it will cultivate their minds, and
quicken and invigorate their understanding.

With this view the following little
work was undertaken: its plan is more
particularly explained in the introductory
conversation.   For obvious reasons, historical or well-authenticated facts have
been selected for the present occasion, in
preference to imaginary descriptions of
moral excellence.

If it shall be objected, that many great
characters, which have, for ages, been
considered as illustrious models of virtue,

are, in this work, treated with too little respect, and their merits too lightly appreciated, the author begs to be understood, that whatever she has said, has been only for the sake of argument; and that no one can entertain a higher opinion of these characters than herself; but, in drawing a comparison between different competitors, it was impossible to show the superiority of one, without pointing out, at the same time, in what the others were inferior.

The parallel between the ancients and the moderns forms only a subordinate part of the plan of the work. On a question, so long agitated by men distinguished for their talents and learning, it would have been the extreme of presumption in

her to attempt to decide. She has not
the vanity to suppose, the question at all
affected by the instances in which she has
assigned the superiority to the moderns;
she only hopes, that her reasons for this
preference will not be found to be altogether without ground, or sophistical.

Brompton,
Dec. 1805.

CHRISTMAS FIRE-SIDE.

AT HOLLY HALL, in the county of Devon,
the family of Arborfield had resided for several
centuries; and had always been remarkable
for maintaining the true English character of
integrity, benevolence, and hospitality. These
good qualities produced the natural conse-
quences, in a place where the innate goodness
of the human heart had not been exposed, as
in great cities, to the allurements of luxury,
or the contagion of vice: and Sir Hubert Arborfield, taking possession of the estate upon
the death of his father, found that, together
with it, he inherited the esteem and love of
all around him. Nor was he of a disposition
to consider this the least valuable part of his
inheritance, nor inclined to part with it to
improve the other. He was the patron of the

industrious, and the father of the distressed;
and his mind was as richly stored with ac-
complishments as his heart with virtues.
While young, he was much attached to the
daughter of a neighbouring gentleman; and
finding, on a long acquaintance, every reason
to consider his attachment well founded, he
married her. This union, which was attended
with more happiness than usually falls to the
lot of humanity, was blessed with a lovely
offspring, two sons and a daughter; who promised to unite, with the graces of the mother,
the excellent qualities of the father. To confirm their natural good dispositions, and un-
fold their youthful talents, was the chief care
and delight of Sir Hubert and his amiable
lady. Their instructions, imparted with tenderness, were received with affectionate respect; and, by a happy mode of blending
amusement with study, they enlightened the
minds of their children without fatiguing them.

At a proper age the sons were sent to
Winchester college; while their sister, remain-
ing under the immediate care of her parents,
received, at home, instructions in the polite
branches of education, from the best masters
the neighbourhood afforded. Their Christmas holidays were always passed at Holly Hall,

at which time their cousins, Jane and Charles Woodley, usually spent a week with them.

It is during one of these festive seasons, when George, the eldest son of Sir Hubert, had reached his fourteenth year, that we propose to introduce this family party to the acquaintance of our young readers. It may not be amiss, however, first to give some idea of their different characters.

With great quickness of parts, George possessed, at the same time, a solidity of judgment; and, with much mildness and generosity, a firmness and prudence not often united. He had, therefore, at school many friends, and no enemies. His brother Edmund, who was two years younger, had an imagination still more lively, but his judgment was not so correct. His disposition partook of the character of his mind: he was high-spirited, generous, brave; but all this was carried to excess; and if it made him more beloved by some than his brother, it also made him less esteemed by others, whose esteem was of more value. Emily Arborfield, who was a year older than Edmund, more resembled George in character, and was beloved equally by them both.

Their cousins were of dispositions not less amiable. Charles possessed much good sense and considerable abilities. His memory was strong, and easily retained what he read or heard. His father died while he was very young; and, in consequence, he became the sole possessor of a very large estate. This might have been the cause of his future misery, instead of happiness, had it not been for the attention of his uncle, Sir Hubert, who took care to have him properly educated, and to remove from him all persons who, to ingratiate themselves, might have flattered him by imprudent indulgencies. Still, however, there were some little foibles in his character, the almost necessary consequence of his situation. His sister Jane was, like him, good tempered, sensible, and accomplished. She was extremely fond of her studies, and loved best to pursue them in company with her cousin Emily; but she was diffident of herself, and particularly reserved in the presence of her uncle, whom she looked up to with a degree of respect bordering upon awe. They all loved each other dearly, and thought no time so agreeable as that which they passed together.

Such was the party assembled at Holly Hall in the Christmas week. Their spirits were enlivened by the festivities of the season, and the happiness which they saw painted on the countenances of all around them; for Sir Hubert kept up the good old English custom, of distributing food and raiment to those who were in need of them, that all might wear the smile of content at a time which, for ages, has been dedicated, by good Christians, to innocent mirth and festivity. On these occasions the young people always acted as Sir Hubert's almoners; and the pleasure, which they evidently felt in dispensing these favours, and the kindness and tenderness of the manner in which they conferred them, gave their worthy parents as much happiness as they bestowed.

In the evening, when the party met round the social fire, after the usual sports, Charles Woodley proposed that they should each tell a story, and, if they pleased, he would begin.

"I will tell you," said he, "such a terrible story about a ghost, that you will be afraid to look round you; I am sure I am very perfect in it, for my servant James told it me the other day, and I have never gone to bed since without thinking of it."

"I do not wish, my dear Charles," said Sir Hubert, "to interfere in your amusements, though, I confess, I do not think there is much amusement in being so terribly frightened as you say we shall be; and though

James is, I believe and hope, a very good and
very honest servant, he is not, perhaps, the
fittest person in the world to afford us either
entertainment or instruction.   At all events,
in the present instance, the subject of his
conversation does not seem to have been very
rational: I think we can employ our time to
more advantage than in talking about ghosts.
I do not wish to mortify your feelings, my
dear Charles, but I would not have you con-
verse with your servants, except on the business for which you employ them.   Always
speak to them with kindness, and treat them
with humanity ; but, as their education has
not fitted them for that rank in society which
you ought to hold, do not you, of your own
accord, reduce yourself to their level; it will
neither make them happy, nor you respect-
able.   I like your proposal of each telling a
story very well; and, if you will allow me to
suggest a hint or two, it may amuse and instruct us at the same time.   I hope you all
recollect the interesting stories you meet with
in the books, which you read at school.   You
find there many examples of generosity, humanity, and other virtues, which, I trust,
made a deep impression on your memory, and
have excited in you a desire to emulate them.

Suppose then, I fix upon some moral excellence, for the subject of our conversation to night: you shall illustrate it by those great examples, which you can recollect from the ancient authors; we will then examine the merits of each instance which you adduce, and decide to which of them most praise is due."

The young friends expressed themselves much pleased with the proposal, and Lady Arborfield suggested, as an improvement, that the young ladies should, on their parts, give anecdotes of the same description from modern history; from whence they might judge of the truth of the assertion, that the ancients were so much more inclined to the practice of virtue than the moderns.

" An excellent idea, indeed!" cried Sir Hubert: " well, then, you shall be the champions for the moderns, and we for the ancients; and I trust we shall have the victory; for our cause, I believe, is best, and we have the advantage of numbers."

"That would be unfair, my dear father," cried George, " particularly as we dispute with ladies; so, if you please, I will not confine myself to either party, but attach myself alternately to that, whose cause I shall think to be most just."

"O, brave!" exclaimed Sir Hubert, "you combat securely, George; if you support that cause which is most just, you will not easily be beaten."

"But, I may be mistaken in my opinion," replied George, "and take the wrong side."

"Well, we will soon try the correctness of your judgment," said Sir Hubert; "suppose then, for this evening, we take the subject of fraternal affection. I know you all love each other dearly, and, therefore, will be pleased with instances of the same affection in others."

The young party looked at each other with a smile sweetly affectionate, which seemed to say, "We do love each other dearly," and all were delighted with the subject proposed.

"Who shall begin?" said Lady Arborfield. "By the laws of courtesy," replied Sir Hubert, "we ought to yield the precedence to you; but we must not sacrifice right to politeness, and the ancients have, undoubtedly, a claim to priority; George, perhaps, has not determined which side he will espouse, and Charles or Edmund, therefore, must begin."

After a short conversation between the two young friends, Edmund entered upon the subject proposed, with the following story.

"The great Cato, who killed himself at Utica, because he would not survive the liberty of his country, had a brother called Cæpio. Being asked, when he was a child, whom he loved best, he replied, 'My dear brother.' He was then asked, who he loved next best, and he made the same answer; and, being desired to say who was the third person in the world that he preferred to all others: he still replied, 'My dear brother.' As he grew older, he still grew fonder, if possible, of Cæpio; and he would neither sup, nor appear in the forum, nor go upon any journey without him. When Cæpio was employed as a military tribune, in some expedition, Cato immediately entered himself a volunteer in the same legion, that he might share his toils, and fight by his side against the enemy. Some time afterwards, (I do not remember how it happened,) they were separated: and Cato was told that his poor brother was taken ill at some town in Thrace. I cannot tell how sorry he was when he heard it. He resolved to fly to his brother instantly; but he was obliged to cross the sea, to go to him. It was a terrible storm, and no ship would venture out. At last, however, he got an open boat, and, attended only by two friends and three faithful slaves, he bravely

quitted the shore. The wind blew, and the
waves rolled terribly; and they thought every
moment that the little boat would be swal-
lowed up. But they were going upon a kind
errand, and the sea and the tempest spared
them; and they reached the shore in safety.
The moment Cato landed, he was told that
his brother was dead. He could not speak
for some time; and though Cato was a Stoic,
(and they say Stoics boasted of the hardness
of their hearts,) he cried as much—as much as
I should, if any misfortune were to happen to
any of you. When his sorrow grew a little
calmer, he celebrated his funeral as splendid-
ly as possible, in the Roman manner, and
erected a beautiful monument, called a Ce-
notaph, to his memory. As he was going to
sail, on his return to Italy, some friends advised him to transport his brother's remains in
another vessel, thinking, perhaps, that the
sight of them only served to keep his grief
alive; but he told them, that he would sooner
part with his life."

"You have made a good beginning, my
dear Edmund," said Sir Hubert, "and now,
Charles, we will trouble you."

Charles reflected a short time, and thus began;

" The story I mean to tell, is of two other Romans, the celebrated Scipios.

"During a war in Asia, with King Antiochus, that province fell to the lot of Lucius Scipio. The Roman senate, who did not think well either of his courage or understanding, wished to give the person who was his colleague in office, the command of the army instead of him. As soon as this was proposed in the senate, the famous Scipio Africanus, who was the elder brother of Lucius, rose up from his seat in great agitation. He assured them, that his brother was a man of more spirit and greater abilities, than they seemed to think; and, to convince them that he thought so, he promised, notwithstanding his age, and the many victories which he had won, and which exempted him from further service, that he would himself attend Lucius into Asia, and serve under him as his lieutenant. The senate were satisfied with this, and Lucius was suffered to take the command: and, by the assistance of his brother, who went with him, as he had promised, he ended the war in such a glorious manner, that he was honoured with a public triumph, and received the name of Asiaticus."

"These Romans were noble fellows, indeed," said Lady Arborfield, when Charles had finished his story; "and a few more such anecdotes as these, would make us believe that they were as virtuous as they were brave. And now, George, which side do you espouse? Are you for the ancients, or cannot you recollect some story as much in favour of the moderns, as those, related by your cousin and brother, are to the honour of the Romans."

" I remember," replied George, "one instance of fraternal affection, which I think very remarkable; but, as I hope my dear father will be kind enough to oblige us, in his turn, with a story, he may, perhaps, anticipate me, and then I must think of another."

" Oh, it is but fair," said Sir Hubert, "that I should tell my story; but, for fear I should happen to fix on the same that you have thought of, you had better begin."

" No, I thank you," answered George, "we will, if you please, go regularly round the circle: so, as you sit next to Charles, pray oblige us with your story first."

" The anecdote I propose to relate," said Sir

Hubert, " is not to be found in the classical histories of Greece, or of Rome; but is recorded by a people, who lay claim to a higher antiquity than any other nation in the world.

" Cucho, an emperor of China, had three sons, and was fonder of the youngest than either of the others; indeed, he carried this partiality so far, that, when he was dying, he declared him his sole successor; excluding his brother from the crown. Besides the injustice of this to his other sons, it was contrary to the laws of the empire; which no king ought to break through upon any account; much less to gratify any views of private interest. Upon the emperor's decease, therefore, the people determined to bestow the crown upon the elder brother, who had the legal right to succeed. This design being universally approved, they prepared to put it into execution; but the elder brother, thanking them for their intentions towards himself, rejected the offer; and, taking the crown, immediately placed it upon the head of his younger brother: publicly declaring, that he thought himself unworthy to wear it, since he had been excluded by his father; who could not now revive, and retract

C

what he had done. His brother, filled with love and admiration at such an extraordinary act of generosity and filial piety, refused the crown likewise, and earnestly entreated him not to oppose the inclination and request of his faithful people: adding, that he alone was the true heir to the kingdom; that he derived his right from a power far superior to the will of their deceased father; that their father was guilty of injustice to the whole nation, when he infringed its laws; that he was betrayed into such a step by a fond partiality which he had not deserved; and that, whether he consented or not, the people had certainly a right to withhold their consent to an act, which tended to destroy the basis of their constitution. Arguments, however, were of no effect: in this strife of love and generosity, neither could prevail; and the people beheld with astonishment and admiration two young princes, when neither could persuade the other to become his sovereign, resign a rich and powerful empire to the second brother, and leave all the splendor of a court, for the pleasure of solitude and fraternal affection."

"Well, you did not think of my story, my dear Sir," said George, when Sir Hubert had ended, "and now, therefore, if you will give me leave, I will tell it myself."

"There was a king, named Antiochus, (I do not recollect where he reigned) who had a brother, to whom he was excessively attached. He was continually doing him all manner of kind offices, and seemed anxious to show him, by all the means in his power, how much he loved him. But Seleucus (that was his brother's name) was as bad and ungrateful as the king was good and affectionate. He was too proud to feel gratitude for all the favours that were heaped upon him; and too ambitious to remain contented, while any one had greater power than himself. The riches and power that were lavished on him by his affectionate brother, served him as the means to raise a rebellion against his throne. Antiochus collected an army, not so much to defend his own private interests, as to preserve from violation the laws of his kingdom. This army soon met the forces which Seleucus had seduced into rebellion. The army of the king had justice on their side, and fought with enthusiasm; while the rebels, only urged on by despair, were soon defeated; and Seleucus was supposed to have perished in the action. When

Antiochus heard this report, instead of re-
joicing for the victory obtained, and the rebellion suppressed, he exclaimed, with tears
in his eyes, "I have preserved my throne, but
I have lost my dear brother!" and immediately laying aside his robes, he put on a mourning
habit, ordered the gates of his palace to be
shut, and gave himself up entirely to grief. It
was, however, soon after discovered, that Seleucus was still alive, and busily employed in
recruiting another army. When the affectionate monarch was informed of this, he was so
transported with joy, that he again appeared
in public, offered sacrifices to the gods for the
happy escape of his brother, and commanded
a general festival, on the occasion, to be kept
throughout his dominions."

"Now, then, we must see," said Lady Arborfield, "what instances we can bring of the
virtue of modern times, in this respect: and,
as it is settled that we must take our turns as
we sit, we will thank you, Jane, to begin."

"The famous John De Witt, the grand
pensionary of Holland," said Jane, after a few
moments of recollection, "was as remarkable
for his love to his brother Cornelius, as for

the other eminent qualities that distinguished him. This tender affection, unfortunately, brought him to a tragical end. When his ungrateful countrymen sentenced his brother to banishment, he went in his own coach to the prison, where he was confined, to carry him out of the town. The people, forgetting the past services of the De Witts, were now as much their enemies as they had once been their friends; and were in hopes that Cornelius would have been put to death, instead of being banished. When the prison gate was opened, it was about the middle of the day; John De Witt came out first, and his brother followed him close; but a woman seeing them, cried aloud to the people, many of whom were watching, armed, about the prison. 'Here come the traitors! kill them! kill them!' Then the sentinels of the prison desired the brothers to go back, or they might be fired upon. John De Witt attempted to speak to the people, but they instantly levelled their muskets at him; so that the brothers were obliged to return into the prison.

"Cornelius now entreated his brother to leave him, and not risk the danger which was threatened. 'They mean no harm to you,' said he; 'it is me alone they hate. Your

high office will protect you from insult, if you
do not irritate them, by showing them that
you still think me worthy of your love. Then,
leave me to my fate, my dear brother, I may
contrive to escape, unobserved: at all events,
let me have the satisfaction to reflect, that I
have not hazarded your life, which is so much
more dear to me than my own.' No entreaties,
however, could prevail upon the affectionate
heart of John De Witt, to desert his unfortunate brother. At length, the people increa-
sing in violence, and urged on by some wicked persons, burst open the prison doors, and
rushed into the room where the two brothers
were. John was found sitting on the bed,
upon which his brother was lying in his night-
gown, reading in a Bible: he asked them what
they wanted, and what was the cause of their
violence. He was answered that they must
go down; he then desired to know what they
meant to do to them; and then they all cried
out, 'To kill you! to kill you!' Whilst he was
speaking, one of the ruffians dragged Cornelius from the bed; when John saw this, and
found that no words could appease the rage
of these men, he took his brother by the hand,
and went with him down stairs. As soon as
he got out of the prison door, he prepared to

address the soldiers, who were assembled there in arms, but was instantly knocked down: as he rose again, he saw that Cornelius was seized, when, hiding his face in his cloak, that he might not behold the murder of a brother whom he so dearly loved, they were both, almost at the same instant, assaulted by several at once, and inhumanly butchered."

"And now," said Lady Arborfield, "as it is my turn, I will relate an anecdote in private life which recently occurred; and which, I confess, I shall feel more pleasure in recounting, as it will show that the virtue of fraternal affection is not solely confined to men. When we were last in town, in a morning visit I made to an old friend, I met a lady, whose gentle manners and amiable countenance particularly engaged my regard. On her taking leave, I could not help expressing my admiration, in very warm terms, to the lady I was visiting. She said she was happy in having it in her power to tell me an anecdote of Mrs. B——, which could not fail to justify the very favourable impression I had already received of her.

"Her uncle," proceeded my friend, "had

amassed a large fortune in the East Indies,
and, not being married, he adopted this lady
and her brother.   The latter, who was a very
amiable young man, was treated and considered as his future heir, nor was there any
doubt of this entertained till within a very
short time of the uncle's death.   Unfortunately Mr. W—— was of a violent and capricious
disposition; and conceiving an unjustifiable
resentment against his nephew, for a very
trifling and unintentional offence, he made
his will, and left the whole of his immense
fortune to his niece.   There are few people,
even of the most generous dispositions, that
would have thought of doing more than di-
viding this bequest with her less-favoured
brother; nor could any one have denied her
the just praise which such a disinterested proceeding would have deserved.   But Mrs. B—
possessed a mind which could not satisfy itself with what she considered a mere act of
justice.   Though she lamented, equally with
her brother, the unfortunate circumstance
which had deprived him of the affection of
their early benefactor; yet, she rejoiced in
the opportunity it gave her of proving the sincerity of her fraternal affection.   She instantly
ordered a deed of gift to be drawn, transferring

the whole of her uncle's property to her brother; reserving only to herself a small estate at
Warfield, in Berkshire, which was endeared to
her by early habits, where she had passed, together with her brother, some of the happiest
years of her life. In vain was every attempt
that he made to decline this noble gift. 'Do
not, my dear brother,' said this charming woman, ' deprive me of the only pleasure my poor
uncle's preference has given me. Before his
death I possessed a fortune sufficient for my
wishes, and if that had not been the case, I could
never have enjoyed possessions which, from a
mere mistake, were withheld from another.'"

"I wish, my dear mother," said Emily,
" that I could recollect some instance of a
lady equally generous and affectionate; but,
as I cannot, I will relate the only story to the
purpose that I can think of at present.

"It was, I believe, some time during the
reign of our Henry VIII. that a Portuguese ship
set sail from Lisbon to Goa, a rich and flourish-
ing colony belonging to that nation, in the
East Indies. There were no less than one hundred persons on board. They had a prosperous
voyage till they had passed the Cape; but, as

they directed their course towards the Indian
Ocean, they discovered in their charts a large
ridge of rocks, which was laid down in the
véry latitude in which they were then sailing.
The captain, therefore, desired the pilot to lie
by in the night, and to slacken sail by day,
till they should be past the danger; but the
pilot, obstinate and unskilful, so far from
complying with the captain's request, actually
crowded more sail than the vessel had carried
before, and, in a few hours, the disaster which
had been apprehended befel them.   The ship
struck upon the ridge of rocks; and it may
easily be imagined the scene of horror this
dreadful   accident   must   have   occasioned
amongst such a number of persons, who had
now nothing before them but the prospect of
instant death.   In this distress the captain ordered the boat to be hoisted out, and taking
the few provisions he could, at such a crisis,
think of, he jumped in first himself, and was
followed by nineteen others, who, with their
drawn swords, prevented any of the rest of
the ship's crew following, lest the boat should
be overset.   In this condition they put to sea,
trusting to that Providence from whom alone
they could hope relief.   Without a compass
to steer by, or a drop of fresh water, they

sailed for four days, scarce able to guess their
course. At length, the captain, who had been
for some time past weak and sickly, sunk exhausted, and expired before their eyes. To
their former miseries was now added the confusion, which naturally ensued, for want of a
commander; every one was desirous to govern, but none inclined to obey. They were
obliged, however, to elect one of the company; and it was agreed that they should, for
the general good, implicitly follow his orders.
They were now reduced to the most dreadful
despair; their small stock of provisions, they
discovered, would not last them more than
three days longer, and it was proposed, by
their new captain, to draw lots, and to cast
every fourth man overboard. Amongst their
small number there was a friar and a carpen-
ter, both of whom they agreed to exempt;
the first from religious motives, and the last
that he might repair the boat, in case of a
leak, or any other accident. They likewise
made the same determination in favour of the
captain, he being the odd man, and his life,
from his superior knowledge, of much consequence to them: this indulgence he would
have refused, but they overcame his objections, and obliged him to acquiesce. There

remained now sixteen, four of whom must,
from dreadful necessity, consent to perish for
the preservation of the rest. Three submitted
to their fate with the greatest resignation,
after having prepared themselves for a future
state; but the fourth was a Portuguese gentleman, who had a younger brother with him
in the boat. This affectionate young man, on
seeing his brother about to be thrown overboard, burst into an agony of grief; and embracing him, entreated that he might die in
his stead. 'Oh, my dear brother!' said he
' consent to my request, and let me have the
satisfaction of dying, to restore a beloved brother to his wife and family. If you refuse my
request, I swear to you, I will not survive the
moment that deprives me of you. Consider
then what is to become of that unhappy family. My life,' continued the generous youth,
' is of no importance: I have no tie strong
enough to bind me to this world, should you
perish; but think of the misery that must en-
sue to that affectionate wife and those dear
children, should you deprive them of their
natural protector by a mistaken tenderness
for me.'—The elder brother resisted his entreaties with all the arguments which affection could devise; but he was deaf to his

remonstrances, and persisted in his determination of sacrificing himself in the stead of his
brother; who, at length, after a severe struggle with his feelings, yielded to the affecting
picture the exemplary youth drew of the distress his family would be involved in, should
he refuse his request. The poor fellow was
then thrown overboard: he was a good swim-
mer, however, and endeavoured to keep himself afloat by seizing the rudder. This being
perceived by one of the sailors, he immediately cut off his right hand with his sword;
the youth sunk for a moment, but, rising again,
he caught the rudder with the other hand;
that received the same fate. He was now deprived of both his hands, but, still feeling a
desire for life, he endeavoured to excite the
compassion of the company, by holding up to
their view his poor bleeding arms. This had
the effect desired; his affecting situation, added
to his noble sacrifice of himself, determined
them in his favour. 'He is but one man,'
said they; 'let us endeavour to save him.'
He was immediately taken into the boat, his
wrists bound up, and all the care taken of him
that the circumstances would permit. Their
humanity met with the reward it deserved: at
sun-rise, to the inexpressible joy of this little

crew, they discovered land, which proved to
be the mountains of Mozambique, in Africa,
and not far distant from a Portuguese colony.
There they all arrived in safety, and continued till the next ship that arrived from Lisbon carried them to Goa."

"And now, then," said Sir Hubert, "to decide which of these instances is most entitled
to our admiration.   We will take them in the
order in which they were told. You will, I suppose, Edmund, defend the hero of your tale."

"Yes," replied Edmund quickly; "for
though Cato had not the same opportunity of
showing his love for his brother as the others
had, I dare say he would have done as much
for him as any of them, if he had been put to
the proof."

"But, my dear brother," said George, "we
are to decide upon the facts as they are related, and not take into consideration what
might have happened in other circumstances."

"But," retorted Edmund, " Cato loved no
one in the world but Cæpio; and he risked
his life, that he might be near him, to be kind
and attentive to him while he was sick."

"That does not prove," said Charles,
"that his love for his brother was greater

than the attachment of his friends, who went with him. So, perhaps, the danger was not so great as it is said to have been."

"Besides," added Emily, "Cato did not set much value upon his life, since he put an end to it himself."

"That was," replied George, " because he would not live a slave, and see good men oppressed by the wicked and tyrannous, without being able to help them."

" You must not suffer your admiration of the Romans, my dear boys," said Lady Arborfield, "to lead your judgment astray in this respect. Suicide is never justifiable. Cato was a brave and a good man; but this act, which is generally considered the greatest proof of his magnanimity, appears to me the greatest instance of his weakness. It seems to have been the effect of despair, rather than of resolution. The only thing that can be said in his favour is, that, as he lived in ages of heathenism, he did not know that it was a crime which he committed."

" Your hero, Edmund," said Sir Hubert, " does not seem likely to bear away the palm of excellence in this contest of affection. He was, however, undoubtedly a most worthy man and most loving brother; and perhaps, as you

say, only wanted an opportunity to give as
striking a proof of his affections as any of those
that have been mentioned."

Edmund looked rather disconcerted, and
seemed unwilling to give up the point, when
Charles observed, that he thought the conduct
of Scipio much more entitled to admiration.
"Scipio," said he, "was an old man; he had
obtained the highest honours his country
could bestow; nothing could add to his fame;
and, to a man like him, honour was much
dearer than life. And yet he risked this honour, and his life too, that his brother might
not be disgraced."

"But he felt," said Edmund, "that he and
his whole family were concerned in the slight
intended to be thrown upon his brother; and,
therefore, it was as much upon his own account as his brother's that he opposed the intention of the senate; and he went with him
to the war, lest he should commit some mistake, and so prove that the senate were right
in their opinion."

"Shrewdly observed, Edmund," said Sir
Hubert; "I perceive you are determined, if
you cannot obtain the palm for your own
hero, that no other shall acquire it easily. In
the instance I repeated to you, can you disco-

ver any circumstance which does not appear
to arise exclusively from fraternal affection?"

"No!" exclaimed Edmund. "No! A
throne is so great a thing. All people are so
fond of ruling. There's Mr. Melville's old
gardener seems to take more pleasure in or-
dering his men about, than in all the flowers
in the garden. And do not you remember,
George, at Winchester, the serjeant we saw
drilling the men, as we went last fifth of No-
vember to St. Catharine's Hill, how proud he
seemed of his place: I am sure he caned some
poor fellows, who did their exercise very well,
only to show his authority. But it is not only
men that are fond of ruling: for there is the
old cock in our poultry-yard that will not let
any other fowl there peck a grain of barley,
or scratch up a worm, but when he pleases,
and where he pleases. The only thing is, my
dear Sir, I do not know which of your king
Cucho's sons to admire most."

"Oh!" cried Jane, who had not yet taken
a part in the dispute, "I should think the
eldest brother is most to be praised, because,
as my uncle says, he had both the law and the
people on his side, and, therefore, it was he
alone that had the crown to give."

"Your observation is extremely just, my

love," said Sir Hubert; "and I am glad to find that you think so correctly. But the merit of the younger brother is not less in another point of view. He was, by the will of his father, in the actual possession of the throne; and a person in that situation, whatever his right may be, will always find people ready to maintain him in it."

"Still, I cannot but think," said George, "that the elder brother deserves our admiration most; because the conduct of the younger was only a consequence of his example. Had he not done so, what respect could he have hoped for from his subjects, after showing himself so much inferior in generosity to the man whom they wished to be their king? It seems too, that both these brothers were good men, and worthy of each other: nor is it said, that the partiality of the father had caused any enmity between them. But, in the example which I brought forward, Antiochus had heaped favours upon his brother, and, in return, had received nothing but ingratitude; and he wept when he believed him killed, though it was in an attempt against his own life; and rejoiced when he found he was still living, though at the same time he knew he was plotting both against his life and throne.

So much better did he love this ungrateful brother than himself."

"You plead your cause well, George," said Sir Hubert; "and this is certainly an extremely strong instance of the force of brotherly love. But, though an amiable man, I am afraid Antiochus was rather a weak one; at all events, he carried his love to his brother to an excess not consistent with the duty he owed to his subjects. As a brother, he might feel happy that his Seleucus had escaped with his life; but, as he was again stirring up rebellion, in which the lives and happiness of thousands of his innocent subjects might be destroyed, it was an insult to them to bid them rejoice for what they must have considered as their greatest misfortune."

"I am afraid," said Jane, "I shall not be able to say as much in favour of my hero as you have of yours; and then John De Witt will not rank so high as he ought to do, because I am unable to place his merit in the best light."

"You are quite a rhetorician, Jane," said Sir Hubert, interrupting her. "It is one of the arts which orators employ, to pretend to inability and want of eloquence, at the very time when they are producing their strongest arguments, clothed in the most beautiful language."

"Is not that speech of Antony's over the dead body of Julius Cæsar, written by Shakespear, one of this sort of masked batteries?" enquired Edmund.

"It is," replied Sir Hubert; "and one of the most beautiful and elegant of the kind: I am glad to find you remember it. But why do you call them masked batteries?"

"Because, in masked batteries, you are attacked from a quarter where you did not expect any harm, and, being unprepared for it, are often conquered. And is not this trick of orators something like it?

"Your metaphor is not quite correct," replied Sir Hubert, "but it is ingenious; and I am happy to see that you reflect on what you read. I was not aware that you knew so much about the art of war: but now let us hear what orator Jane has to say for her grand pensionary."

"Oh, now you are laughing at me, my dear uncle," said Jane, smiling; but you will all allow that life is the dearest thing we have, and the last we are willing to part with; and yet John De Witt lost his for the sake of his brother."

"Not exactly so," said Charles; "because when he went to the prison it was noon day, and that was not a time he would have chosen to attempt to carry him out of the town, if he had thought that the citizens had any de-signs against his life."

"But he found that they had," answered George, "when they were obliged to return into the prison on account of the threats of the people; and, therefore, if he had not been determined to hazard all events for the sake of his brother, he might have left him then."

"But perhaps he thought," replied Charles, "that whatever their designs were against his brother, they had none against himself; and he might suppose too, as he was still in office, that they would pay too much respect to his authority to offer him any insult."

"No: that is taking away all merit from him at once," said Edmund, "and does not seem to be very likely neither; because, when they came out of the prison, the people threat-ened him as well as his brother, and would not listen to him, though he attempted to speak to them several times."

"You are very gallant, my dear boys," said Lady Arborfield, "to espouse thus the young lady's cause. But I do not think it is an easy question to decide; in all cases, however, where two opinions can be formed, we should always take that which is most favourable to the person, who is the subject of them. I will leave you to discuss the merits of the anecdote, which I repeated to you, though, I confess, I do not think it approaches to a level with several of those, which we have already considered."

"I am glad you say so yourself, mamma," said Emily; "for though it was a generous action in Mrs. B——— to give so large a fortune to her brother, it was what she did not want, and what she considered he had a juster claim to than herself."

"Oh, money!" cried Edmund, "I should not think a person generous because he gave a great deal of money; and, I am sure, I should love any one better, who would be sorry when I was unhappy, than any other, who should give me as much as the great diamond was worth, that Mr. Pitt's great grandfather sold to the king of France."

"You must not speak too lightly of money neither," said Sir Hubert. "You are not yet capable of judging of its value; and though it may be pleasant to have a friend to sympathize with you in distress, yet if you and your friend were cold and hungry, and had not a farthing of money to buy you any food, you would then find the misery of your friend only an aggravation of your own. Money, my dear Edmund, is a valuable possession, if we know how to use it rightly: it affords us the means of conferring happiness on others, and by so doing increases our own. And now it gets rather late, we must conclude our argument as soon as we can; but we must hear Emily's arguments in favour of her young Portuguese."

"Really," said Emily, "my cousin and brothers are so quick at making objections, that I do not know how I shall defend myself against them; and yet I cannot think what they can suggest to lessen the merit of the action. He sacrificed his life for his brother, after he had stood an equal chance by lot. It cannot be said, as it was of John De Witt, that he did not know his danger, because the danger was before his eyes, and he had seen three drowned already. Nor that, like Cato, he was a heathen, and did not know the value of life; for he said his prayers with the priest, and received absolution from him before he was thrown overboard. Nor can it be said that, in the miserable situation to which they were reduced, he thought death preferable to life, for he attempted to save himself by swimming; not repenting of the sacrifice he had made, but, no doubt, in the hope of being saved by some vessel, which might pass that way, or of being floated by the waves to land."

" You have anticipated all objections, I believe, Emily," said her father.

"No!" cried Edmund, "there is one, which Emily has not thought of. It seems that he repented of what he had done, because, when his hands were cut off, he held up his bleeding arms, as if to entreat them to take him again into the boat."

"But they had then deprived him of the power of swimming any longer," said George, " and so destroyed his hopes of any other succour."

" Well, then, Emily," said Sir Hubert, " I think we must resign the palm of victory to your hero, and admit that this modern has, in this one instance, excelled all the ancients, who are distinguished by their fraternal affection. We have, indeed, for the sake of argument and comparison, exerted our ingenuity to discover, in every instance, some circumstance that may be supposed to have influenced the conduct of these celebrated persons, and so

far lessen their merit. By which you will perceive, how much easier it is to depreciate, than
to imitate excellence; for all these persons
were, undoubtedly, extremely amiable, and
have justly been held up as models of fraternal affection; but as, in every thing else, there
are regular degrees and gradations, so some of
these are distinguished by stronger characters
of virtue than the rest."

"If you have received as much pleasure
in this mode of passing our time, as you have
given me, we will amuse ourselves, to-morrow
evening, in the same manner; and, that you
may not be unprepared, (though, from the
proof you have given to-night of your memory
and judgment, I have no reason to suppose
you will), you shall chuse your own subject to-
night."

The young people scarcely hesitated a
moment, but exclaimed, almost with one
voice, "Filial Affection shall be our subject
to-morrow night; and we will see, if any one
ever loved their parents better than we do our
dear father and mother."

THE next evening, our young friends left off their sports earlier than usual, and, forming a close circle round the fire, seemed anxious to enter upon the subject proposed for discussion.

Sir Hubert perceived their thoughts by the animation of their looks: "I see," said he, "that you are prepared, and eager to commence our instructive amusement; and, as one striking exemplification of the subject you have chosen, has occurred to my memory, I will lead the way.

"Among the many persons, who were proscribed at Rome, under the triumvirate of Antony, Lepidus, and Octavian (afterwards called Augustus,) were the celebrated orator Cicero and his brother Quintus. As soon as they heard of the fate that was reserved for them, they endeavoured to make their escape to Brutus, who was then at the head of an army in Macedon. The two brothers, who were extremely fond of each other, travelled together some time, mutually condoling their common misfortune: but as they had left Rome in great haste, they were not furnished either with money, or other necessaries for their voyage. It was agreed, therefore, that Cicero should make what haste he could to the sea-side, to secure their passage, while Quintus should return home to procure what they should want. Some of his servants, however, were treacherous, and his return was immediately known; and the house was instantly filled with soldiers and assassins, employed by the triumvirate. Quintus concealed himself so effectually, that the soldiers could not find him. Enraged at their disappointment, they put his son, who was quite a youth, to the torture, in order to make him discover the place of his father's concealment; but filial affection was stronger in the young Roman than the sense of pain. The most exquisite torments could only extort from the generous youth a sigh, and sometimes a deep groan. His agonies were increased by every inhuman mode their cruel ingenuity could suggest: but he still persisted in his resolution, not to betray his father. From the place where Quintus was

concealed, he heard all that passed; and none
but a father can conceive how his heart must
have been agonized by the sighs and groans
of an amiable son, expiring in horrid tortures,
and all to save his life. He could bear it no
longer; he rushed from the place of his concealment; in an agony of grief, scarce able to
speak for tears, he presented himself to the
assassins: ' Take my life,' cried he, ' but spare
my innocent! my glorious boy! The triumvirs
themselves, when they hear his generous conduct,—yes, even they will think him worthy
of reward and approbation.' The inhuman
monsters beheld with unconcern the tears of
a father imploring for his child; and the virtue of the child, dying to save his father.
They answered, that both must die; the father, because he was proscribed, and the son,
because he had concealed his father. Then a
new contest of tenderness arose, who should
die first; but this the assassins soon decided,
by beheading them both at the same instant."

This story, repeated by Sir Hubert in a
tender and impressive manner, drew tears
from all the party; and it was not till after
some moments silence, that Edmund, whose
turn it was to tell the next anecdote, recover-

ed spirits to begin. " What I am going to relate," said he, " happened some years after
this, when Antony and Augustus had quarrel-
led, and were as eager to kill one another, as
they had once been to kill other people.

" After the great battle of Actium, where
Antony was entirely defeated, Augustus held
a council, to examine and condemn the prisoners he had taken. Among the rest, there
was brought before him an old man, called
Metellus. He was very old indeed, and very
weak and unwell, and his beard and hair were
long and matted with filth. His clothes were
extremely ragged, and hardly enough to keep
him from the cold. He was a most miserable
object; and, if I had been Augustus, I should
have pitied him, rather than have been angry
with him. It happened, that the son of this
Metellus was one of the officers of Octavius,
and one of the judges upon this occasion; but,
at first, he did not know his father, in the deplorable condition in which he saw him. At
last, however, recollecting his features, he sprang
from his seat, and running to embrace him, fell
on the poor old man's neck, and cried bitterly.
As soon as he was able to speak, he turned
round to the tribunal, where Augustus sat.

'Cæsar,' said he, 'my father has been your enemy, and I your officer; he deserves to be punished, and I to be rewarded; all that I ask is,
save him, on my account, or order me to be put
to death with him.' All the judges were touched with compassion, at this affecting scene;
Augustus himself relented, and granted to old
Metellus his life and liberty."

"Oh! what a dreadful surprise it must
have been to this young man," said Charles,
"to see his poor old father brought a prisoner
before him, and in such a wretched state!
Had I been in his situation, I do not think I
should have been able to have spoken a word,
I should have been so much affected."

"And then you would not have been able
to have made such an affecting appeal as this
worthy son did, in behalf of his father," said
Sir Hubert; "and this, my dear boy, should
teach you not to sink under any misfortune
that may befall you, but to strive, rather to
strengthen your mind, that you may be able
to make the necessary exertions, to save your
friends or yourself from impending evil."

Charles thanked his uncle for this affectionate and salutary advice, and proceeded with
the following story :

"Bareas Soranus, an illustrious Roman,
distinguished for his vigilance and justice in
the discharge of his duty, was (amongst many
other great and virtuous men) under a false
accusation, put to death, to gratify the cruel
disposition of that monster of iniquity, Nero.
He had a daughter, named Servilia, who was
under the greatest affliction for the misfortunes
of her father. During his confinement, she
was apprehended, and brought into the senate,
and there arraigned. The crime she was accused of was, that she had sold all her jewels
and ornaments, and spent the money, which
she had procured by the sale of them, in con-
sulting magicians. At the mention of this
circumstance, the young Servilia burst into a
flood of tears. 'If this be a crime,' said she,
'then I am indeed guilty. But, could I think
it criminal to search into the fate of a beloved
and unfortunate father? Till he was afflicted,
I did not know that such persons as magicians
existed. I wished to know whether the senators would protect my indulgent parent
against the malice of his false accusers; and,
it was for this purpose that I gave them those
jewels and ornaments, which were no longer
of any value to me: and, oh!' said she, 'how
gladly would I give them my blood and life,

would my blood and life restore my adored father his liberty; but, however criminal you may think this proceeding, I alone am the delinquent; my father was an utter stranger to it. Do not, therefore, I implore you, involve him in my guilt.' I am sorry," said Charles, "that my story has such a melancholy end; instead of acting as the judges of Metellus did, and saving the father, as a reward for the affectionate conduct of his child, they condemned, and put her to death, at the same time with Bareas."

"What an interesting and affecting story you have told, Charles," said Emily, "and, what an innocent and amiable young woman does Servilia appear, while she is making her defence to the senators!"

"Yes," cried Edmund, "and, what inhuman and hard-hearted wretches the senators must have been, not to have felt any compassion for her distress! I do think that I could walk a hundred miles to see such savages suffer death."

"Do not, my love," said Lady Arborfield, "suffer your generous indignation, at the cruelty of others, betray you into a spirit of revenge; but leave to a higher tribunal that

punishment which crimes are ultimately sure
to meet."

"It seems," said George, "that I took the
wrong side last night; but the triumph of the
ladies was so much the greater. I shall not,
therefore, in future, pretend to decide before-
hand on the superior claims of either party to
victory; but will relate whatever anecdote
may occur to me on the subject, which shall
be proposed, without regarding whether it is
in favour of the ancients, or of the moderns.
The one that I recollect at present, however,
is in favour of the former."

"Titus Manlius, the Roman dictator, having exercised great violence and cruelty over
the citizens, was cited, at the expiration of his
office, to answer for his conduct. Among other
things that were laid to his charge, he was accused of treating with barbarity, one of his own
sons. Manlius, it seems, had no other cause of
complaint against him than his having an impe-
diment in his speech, or as some say, a want of
eloquence. For this reason he was banished far
from the city, from his home, and the company
of young men of his own age and fortune; and
condemned to servile works, and a prison, like
a slave. All were highly exasperated against

so severe a dictator, and so inhuman a father,
except the son himself; who, moved with filial
piety, and, under the greatest concern that he
should furnish matter of accusation against
his father, resolved upon a most extraordinary
method to relieve him.   One morning, without apprising any body, he came to the city,
armed with a dagger; and went directly to
the house of the tribune Pomponius, who had
accused his father. Pomponius was yet in bed.
Young Manlius sent up his name, and was immediately admitted by the tribune, who did
not doubt but he was come to discover to him
some new instance of his father's severity.
After they had saluted each other, young Manlius desired a private conference; and, as soon
as he saw himself alone with the tribune, he
drew out his dagger, presented it to his breast,
and declared he would stab him that moment,
if he did not swear, in the form he should dic-
tate, ' Never to hold the assembly of the
people, for accusing his father.' Pomponius,
who saw the dagger glittering at his breast,
himself alone, without arms, and attacked by
a robust young man full of a bold confidence in his own strength, took the oath demanded of him; and afterwards confessed,
with a kind of satisfaction, and a sincerity,

which sufficiently proved he was not sorry for what he had done, that it was that violence, which obliged him to desist from his enterprize. The Roman people were so much pleased with the dutiful and resolute behaviour of young Titus, that, at the ensuing election, they broke through an established custom, and made him second military tribune, though he had yet had no opportunity of signalizing himself in the service of his country."

"I think," said Edmund, when George had finished his story, "that, if young Manlius was not very eloquent, he proved by his conduct, that he wanted neither sense nor courage, as well as affection; for, I remember reading, in Mr. Adam's account of the law proceedings of the Romans, that it was one of the methods practised by accused persons, when they thought they were likely to be found guilty, to prevail upon the accuser to drop the prosecution; and this they did, generally, by the interest of friends, or by bribes: but young Manlius acted a much nobler part. Well, I do not think, that the moderns are likely to get the victory this time, for I cannot conceive any stronger instances of filial affection, than those we have recited."

" I admire your enthusiasm, my dear Edmund," said Lady Arborfield, " as it is in a
generous cause; but do not judge too hastily.
I am willing to think, and I would have you
think so well of human nature, that I would not
set any imaginary bounds to human virtue.   I
read, a short time since, in the annals of Europe, for the year 1740, the story of a young
sailor, whose filial duty, though not so remarkable, certainly, as those of your favourite Romans, made a considerable impression on me."

" It was in very stormy weather, that a
North Carolina ship, laden with tobacco, was
driven full against the white cliffs that lie
at the west end of the Isle of Wight, and
rested her head on a rock, where she continued about an hour, and then broke to pieces.
The captain, yielding to despair, leaped overboard the moment the ship struck, and was
seen no more.   The bowsprit was jammed
into the rock, and formed a sort of bridge to a
shelf in the cliff. Upon this shelf the men got,
and continued in this miserable situation till
day light.   The raging seas below, and above
steep high cliffs hanging over their heads,
how can I describe the horrors of their condition!   Every instant in dread of being dashed

to pieces against the rocks; or, if they escaped
this termination of their miseries, the scarcely
less melancholy one of perishing with hunger,
awaited them. The only hope that remained
was, that the storm might abate, and some
boat might appear in sight, in time to save
them. Among them was a youth, who, in ad-
dition to his own misfortunes, had the torture
of seeing an aged father perishing with cold
and fatigue before his eyes. Worked up to
the greatest pitch of agony, at the sufferings
of a beloved parent, he conceived the desperate resolution of instantly attempting to procure him relief, though he was sure that it was
next to impossible, that he should not perish
in the attempt. The whole crew, even in
their own deplorable state, trembled at the
almost certain fate of this affectionate youth,
and entreated him, with tears, to desist from
his enterprize, and wait the chance of assistance from any boat that might pass. The afflicted parent, feeble as he was, clasped the
knees of his child, and implored him not to risk
his own life, by an attempt to save his, in which
there was more danger, than prospect of success.
' While there is the least prospect of saving
your precious life,' cried the generous youth,
' can you think, my dear father, that any fear

F

for my own, can prevent me from attempting
it? No: I will die, or save you.' At these
words, he strained the weeping old man to his
breast, and then prepared for his enterprize.
The terrors of a tempestuous sea, foaming and
beating against the rocks, which were almost
perpendicular, did not dismay him. He desired to be let down into the raging waves,
which they effected by some small lines, that
they had with them. It was wonderful he was
not instantly dashed to pieces; but the hand
of Providence guided the waves, which bore
him round a point of the cliff, to a low place
on the shore, more than a quarter of a mile
distant from the fatal rock. He immediately
hastened to collect people, whom he led to
the cliff, which overhung the place where the
ship-wrecked crew were expecting that death,
which had long seemed inevitable; for they
had not had the satisfaction of seeing that the
brave youth had succeeded in his attempt to
reach the shore. They were all drawn up by
ropes, by the people above; and, in returning
thanks to Heaven for their miraculous escape,
they did not forget to pray for every blessing
on the youth, whose high sense of filial duty
had enabled him to conquer, what had to
them appeared insurmountable difficulties,

to rescue his aged parent from an untimely
death."

" What a dreadful state," said Emily,
" must the poor old man have been in, whilst
his son was seeking relief for him. I do not
know which I was most alarmed for, whilst
you were telling that part of the story; for, I
am sure the agitation of the father must have
been attended with as much hazard to his life,
as his son encountered from the rocks and
tempestuous waves."

"Indeed, my dear child," said Sir Hubert,
" I am perfectly of your opinion in this respect; but, when the danger was over, how
must the father have gloried in this brave and
affectionate boy, and how justly was his gallant conduct rewarded by the success of his
enterprize! My dear children, ever remember
that, the obligations of a child to a parent
cease but with existence: and, that nothing
will afford you more satisfaction in the decline
of life, than the recollection of never having
been deficient in this, the most important duty
of it."

The glistening eyes of the young party,
convinced Sir Hubert that the lesson was not
lost; and, when he had given a few minutes

to their feelings, he called on Jane for her contribution to the evening's entertainment. She obeyed him, by recounting the following interesting anecdote.

"As some Christian captives at Algiers, who had been ransomed, were going to be discharged, the cruisers brought in a Swedish vessel, among the crew of which was the father of one of those ransomed captives. The son made himself known to the old man; but their mutual distress, at meeting in such a place, may well be conceived. The young man, however, reflecting, that the slavery his father was about to undergo, would inevitably put an end to his life, requested that he might be released, and himself detained in his room; which was immediately granted: but, when the story was told to the governor, he was so affected with it, that he caused the son likewise to be discharged, as the reward of his filial and exemplary tenderness."

"I hope you will not think that I am judging the question before-hand;" said Emily, "when I declare, that, of all the models of filial affection, I have ever read or heard of, the Countess de Villelume holds the most honourable place. She is, I believe, still living, and is now about eight and thirty years old. You have often repeated her story, my dear mamma; and I wonder you did not chuse it for the present occasion yourself. But I do not believe that either my brothers or cousins have heard it; and I will tell it, therefore, for I love to repeat her name."

"The Countess de Villelume is the daughter of General de Sombreuil, who, in the beginning of the French revolution, was governor of the Invalids at Paris. In this post he showed so much attachment to his king, and such strict attention to his duty, and his manners were altogether so amiable, and his character so worthy, that, for some time, even the enemies of the king treated him with respect. But when the furious rebels had got into complete possession of all authority, they seemed to delight in every sort of cruelty and wickedness; and they dragged the poor general, who was seventy-two years old, out of his house, and shut him up in the prison of the Abbey. This was on a Sunday, while his daughter was at church. On her return, hearing what had happened, she immediately flew to the Abbey, but was refused admittance. She, therefore, wrote a petition to the people in power, entreating them to confine her with her father. At the top of this petition the ferocious Marat wrote, 'Confine this aristocratical fanatic with her aristocratical father. With this permission in her hand, she again presented herself before the gates of the Abbey, which were opened to her; in an instant she was in the arms of her dear father. With him she passed her whole time: her days and her nights were spent in serving and consoling him.

"On the terrible second of September, when the general massacre of prisoners began, Mademoiselle de Sombreuil had been confined eight days. After many of these unfortunate victims had been butchered, and the sight of blood, flowing in torrents, only served to inflame the rage of the murderers; while the wretched inhabitants of the prison endeavoured to hide themselves from impending slaughter, this filial heroine rushed into the presence of the assassins, who had already seized General de Sombreuil:—' Monsters!' cried she, 'hold your hands! he is my father.'—She threw herself at their feet, bathed in human gore, and laid hold of their hands, yet reeking with blood. At one moment she

stopped the sword lifted against her father,
and offered herself to its relentless point, ex-
claiming, ' Strike, barbarians! you cannot
reach my father but through my heart. My
body shall cover him: I disdain unworthy
supplications; I desire, I demand only to die
with him.' In this glorious struggle she received five wounds.

"So much courage and filial affection, in
a young and beautiful girl, for a moment ar-
rested the attention of the assassins. She
perceived that they hesitated, and she endeavoured to increase the impression she had
made. But while she was thus trembling between hope and fear, one of the monsters,—
Oh, I shall never forget his name!—Van
Damme—proposed the following condition for
saving the general's life: ' *Drink*,' said the
horrid wretch, ' *a glass of human blood and
save your father.*' The heroic girl shuddered,
trembled, and retreated some paces; but she
forgot terror, disgust, every thing upon earth
but her father, and yielded to the dreadful
condition. ' Innocent or guilty then,' exclaimed one of those who acted as judges,
' it is unworthy of a great and generous nation, and a humane people, to bathe their
hands in the blood of the old man, since they

must first destroy this virtuous girl.' A general cry of pardon was heard. The daughter,
revived by this signal of safety, threw herself
into her father's trembling arms, who had
scarcely power to press her to his bosom;
and even the most outrageous of the assassins
were unable to restrain their tears. Her de-
parture from this place of horrors was a tri-
umphal procession; she beheld the hands,
dyed with the gore of a thousand victims,
that a moment before were ready to be steeped
in her own and her dear father's blood, now
opening a passage for them through a ferocious crowd, panting for carnage; and she
heard these words repeated from every side:
'Let old age and beauty be respected by
all.'"

"I am really inclined to think," said Sir
Hubert, "that the moderns will prove victo-
rious again to-night; but we must not resign
the palm without a struggle. I believe, however, the contest will chiefly rest between
young Cicero and the Countess de Villelume;
but I must not prejudge the question. Who
will undertake the cause of young Cicero?"

"I do not think he needs any one to undertake his cause, my dear Sir," replied Ed-

mund; " his merits are conspicuous enough,
from the story which you were so good as
to repeat to us, and do not stand in need of
any observations to make them appear greater.
What could be more noble, or more disinterested, than his patiently suffering such horrid tortures to save the life of his father?
Metellus certainly showed great filial affection; but how could he well do otherwise
than he did? Could he sit in judgment and
doom his father to death? The manner in
which he conducted himself on the occasion,
and his appeal to Cæsar, were very affecting
no doubt; and his offer to die with his father
proved that he was sincere. But I will not,
because I told the story, attempt to rank him
above those, who, I feel, are entitled to greater
approbation."

"That is a generous sentiment, my dear
boy," said Lady Arborfield; "and does you
more credit than you would have gained by
your ingenuity, in supporting a weak argument against the conviction of your judgment.
But will our friend Charles, to whom we
must confess ourselves obliged for exerting
his memory in favour of our sex, as readily
give up the pretensions of his heroine?"

"Yes," replied Charles, "I am very ready

to follow the example of my cousin. We are pleased with Servilia, and we love her for her simplicity and tenderness; but there is nothing in her conduct so much to excite our admiration as our pity."

" You are very generous," replied George, " but you do not support the character of advocates: but, I confess, I am too partial to my hero to desert him so readily. I think young Titus Manlius deserves, at least, to have his merits placed in as striking a point of view as my abilities will enable me to do."

" Oh, George!" cried Edmund, "I see what you mean to do; you are going to show us that you can make, as Milton says, ' The worse appear the better reason;' and you want to puzzle us to find arguments to refute your ingenious sophistry. But you will not persuade us, with all your ingenuity, that you are sincere in your defence, because we know that you are Mr. Infallible."

George smiled at this sally of his brother's, and replied, "If you do not think I can support his superiority with justice, let us argue in another way, and hear what are your objections."

" Why that is rather an ungracious office," answered Edmund. " As I said before, I

think young Manlius a very noble fellow;
but what sacrifice did he make for his father?
Perhaps, you will say, he sacrificed his resentments. No, you will not say that neither;
because I know you love our dear father and
mother so much yourself, that you never
would suppose any son could feel resentment
against a parent."

George pressed the hand of his brother
affectionately; and Sir Hubert and his lady
looked on them with a sweet smile of tenderness and approbation.

" I do not wish to detract from the merit
of Titus," said Charles, " but as you challenge us to make objections, we may observe,
that, to save the life of his father, he threat-
ened the life of another fellow-creature; and,
to perform his own duty, made another take
an oath to desert what he thought to be
his."

"That is justly remarked," said Sir Hubert; "and it must be farther admitted, that
though his motives were honourable and
praise-worthy, yet the means he took to obtain them tended to intercept the course of
justice; and he sacrificed, therefore, to his
own private feelings, the interests and welfare
of the public at large, which is always most

intimately concerned in the preservation of
their laws, and the due administration of justice towards all, from the dictator to the
meanest slave. Still Manlius is highly entitled
to our praise and admiration. If he did not feel
any resentment against his father for his cruel
and unjust conduct towards him, it was not
much to be expected, that he would exert
himself so actively in favour of one, who
seemed inclined to break the bond which so
sweetly unites a parent to his child; and
whose example, therefore, might have taught
him to look on it with equal indifference. The
Romans showed, by their conduct, that they
had a just sense of his merit: and now, my
dear George, what shall we say farther in his
favour?"

" You have said every thing, Sir, much
better than I could; and I have nothing to
add."

" Since candour seems to be the order of
the evening," said Lady Arborfield, " I will
admit, that my young sailor must not venture
a competition with such exalted characters as
young Cicero and the Countess de Villelume;
nor is it necessary to say any thing to detract
from his merit, for the purpose of making the
comparison more striking."

"If you will not say any thing more, my dear aunt, in favour of your heroic sailor," said Jane, "how shall I pretend to make a panegyric upon my ransomed slave? and yet, I think, there was something uncommonly affectionate in his conduct. He had experienced all the horrors of slavery among those barbarous Moors. He was upon the point of returning to his native country, to his home, and his heart was full of that joy, which animated the spirits of those who had been ransomed with him. To resign all this happiness at once, to return again to the misery he had so long languished under, and all to save his father from those horrors of which he had himself so bitter an experience, was no common sacrifice."

"You have painted the merits of the young Swede in such strong colours," said Sir Hubert, "that, I believe, we must admit him into a glorious triumvirate, (if I may be allowed the expression, where a lady is one of the three,) with young Cicero and the Countess de Villelume. We will not trouble you, my dear Emily, for any eulogy on this incomparable woman. I do not doubt your abilities; but her heroic conduct soars so far

G

above all praise, that we might as well attempt to extol the lustre of the sun in its me-
ridian brightness. She is the glory of her
sex and of our age. She is the first of filial
heroines, may she be the happiest of mothers!"

"I THINK," said Sir Hubert, when the party met the next night, "that humanity was the chosen theme of this evening; and, as there are few topics, I believe, in ancient or modern history, which furnish us with so many incidents, I have no doubt of being as highly entertained, as we have been on the two evenings already passed. We meet with a striking instance in the history of the Athenians, how much this virtue was esteemed by them.

"The senate of the Areopagi, being assembled together on a mountain, without any roof but heaven, a poor little sparrow fled into the bosom of one of the senators, to save itself from a bird of prey, by which it was closely pursued. This man, who was naturally cruel, seized the poor little trembling creature, and dashed it on the ground so roughly, that he killed it. At this, the court was so much offended, that they passed a decree, which banished him from the senate. These judges,

at that time, the most celebrated in the world,
meant to show, by this resentment of cruelty
even to a sparrow, that clemency and a merciful disposition were so necessary in a state,
that a man, destitute of them, was not worthy
to hold any place in the government; having,
as it were, renounced humanity.

" Having said thus much of the virtue itself, I must add, that, if you shall be as much
gratified in hearing, as I have been in reading,
the anecdote I am about to relate, I may, with
confidence premise, that I shall not be deficient in my contribution to the general amusement.

" When the province of Azazene was ra-
vaged by the Romans, seven thousand Persians were brought prisoners to the city of
Amida; where, having nothing of their own
to subsist on, they were exposed to the ex-
tremity of want. Acases, the bishop of the
place, being touched with their distresses, assembled the whole body of his clergy, and represented to them the deplorable condition of
the poor captives, in the most pathetic language, that eloquence could supply. He then
observed, that, as the Almighty preferred
mercy to sacrifice, he would be much better

pleased with the relief of their unfortunate fellow-creatures, than with being served in the golden and silver vessels of their churches. The clergy embraced his proposal, not only with readiness, but with the highest applause; and, having maintained the Persians, during the war, by the sale of the consecrated vessels, they sent them all home, at the conclusion of the peace, with a sufficient sum of money to subsist them on the road. Varanes, the Persian monarch, was so much charmed with this extraordinary act of humanity, that he invited the bishop to his capital; where he received him with the most profound reverence and respect; and, at his request, bestowed many privileges on his Christian subjects, which they had never enjoyed before."

"What a good man must that bishop have been," said Jane, "how I should have loved him: do you think there are many such bishops now?"

"I hope there are," answered Lady Arborfield. "I think with you, my dear, that the bishop of Amida was a most exemplary character, and his conduct, in this instance, must have tended to increase the numbers of converts to christianity; for those heathens, whom

he succoured, could not do otherwise than
think well of a religion, which impelled its
ministers to such disinterested acts of humanity; and it is not likely they were silent on
the occasion."

"Jane asked you, mamma," said Edmund,
"whether you thought there were many such
bishops now; which recalled to my memory,
what I have somewhere read, that there is an
order of priests in Spain, who regularly go
once a year to Algiers, to redeem the captives
in that city: this shows that the same spirit of
humanity still exists. I shall now," continued
he, "till you an instance of this virtue in a
general, which I hope you will think a proof,
that a soldier can sometimes be as humane as
a priest.

"When Quintus Cæcilius Metellus, the
Roman proconsul, had besieged Nertobrigia,
a town in Spain, a chief lord of the country,
named Rhetogenes, was so great a coward as
to leave his wife and children in the city, and
surrender himself to the Romans. The town
was reduced to great distress, and Metellus,
having effected a breach in the wall, had just
ordered a general assault. The inhabitants of
the place, in revenge of the desertion of Rhe-

togenes, placed his wife and children in the
breach, where the Roman legions were about
to mount. The miserable Rhetogenes saw,
with despair, the destruction which threatened them. Metellus too, beheld them; and beheld them with pity. He commanded his soldiers to halt; and had the humanity to relin-
quish a certain conquest, rather than spill the
blood of these innocent victims. He immediately raised the siege, but his humanity received a glorious and just reward; for the
fame of it spread so rapidly, and excited such
admiration through all Terraconian Spain, that
the inhabitants of all the revolted cities were
eager to yield submission to him, and contend-
ed who should be the first. Metellus received
them, and, among the rest, the Nertobrigians,
into an alliance with Rome, and at length re-
covered the whole country."

"I always love," said Emily, "to hear of
tenderness and humanity in soldiers or sailors,
as I think it is more amiable in them than in
others; for, certainly, their being engaged in
continual scenes of warfare, might be supposed to lessen their horror of shedding blood,
did we not continually read of their noble forbearance."

"And, in the present case," said Sir Hubert, "it was, indeed, conspicuously eminent, as this worthy general, by his aversion to shedding the blood of innocent objects, might have subjected himself to disgrace and punishment; but, fortunately, the action procured him a more brilliant victory than he could otherwise have hoped, and that one, which must have been the most grateful to his feelings, as it was a bloodless one."

"I shall," said George, "side with the moderns to-night, so Charles, you will be kind enough to favour us with your story first."

This he did, in the following words:

"Pyrrhus, king of Epirus, having put to flight the army of Antigonus, king of Macedon, seized on his kingdom; but Antigonus soon rallied his loyal troops, and met the army of his ferocious rival at Argos. The inhabitants being much alarmed, sent deputies, entreating that neither of them would enter the city. This request was agreed to: but Pyrrhus treacherously broke his word, and, in the night, rushed with his forces into the town. The inhabitants, in the greatest alarm and confusion, sent to Antigonus, and implored his assistance against a perfidious enemy. He im-

mediately flew to relieve them; and a desperate battle ensued in the streets of the city.
In the morning, it was discovered, that Pyrrhus had received the reward, which his dishonourable conduct deserved; for his body was
found amongst the slain. Alcyoneus, the son
of Antigonus, thinking to please his father,
by convincing him of the death of his enemy,
severed the head of Pyrrhus from the body,
and seizing it by the hair, rode full speed
with it, in search of Antigonus. He found
him in conversation with some of his friends;
and, with a smile of triumph, threw it at his
feet. Antigonus shuddered at the sight of the
head, which he recollected in death; and,
shocked at the savage ferocity of his son,
struck him with his batoon, and, casting on
him a look of contempt, exclaimed, ' Barbarous wretch! how canst thou think that he,
whose grandfather was slain, and whose father died a captive, should rejoice at such a
sight?' Then shedding a flood of tears, he took
the robe from his own shoulders, and covering
the head, ordered his attendants to make strict
search for the body; and that, when it was found,
they should be burnt together, with all the
funeral honours due to a king. Alcyoneus,
abashed and self-condemned, was retiring from

the presence of his father, when he perceived
Helenus, the son of Pyrrhus, disguised in a
miserable and tattered garment. Taking him
by the hand, and addressing him in the kind-
est and most soothing terms, he presented him
to his father. 'Well, my son,' said Antigonus, ' this is better than you did before; but,
you have done less than your duty still, in having suffered a person of his dignity to approach me, in that wretched dress; which is
not a disgrace to him, but to our victory.' He
then condoled with Helenus, on the loss of his
father; entertained him kindly, and, generously restoring him to liberty, sent him home to
Epirus."

"How ashamed must Alcyoneus have
been," said Edmund, "at the rebuke he met
with from his father, when he had flattered himself that he should receive praise. I think he
ought to have been more severely punished for
his barbarity."

"You forget," said Sir Hubert, "his com-
punction for his fault, and his eagerness to
atone for it, in the manner, which he conceived
would be most pleasing to his father; and I
am inclined to think, Edmund, by his conduct,
in that instance, that he was sufficiently

punished by the mode which his father adopted."

"Indeed, my dear father," said Edmund, "I spoke, as I too often do, without sufficient reflection; as I am sure, I know by my own feelings, that the displeasure of an indulgent parent is a severer punishment than any other that can be inflicted."

Sir Hubert received this affectionate confession of his open-hearted boy with an approving smile, and Emily Arborfield took up the cause of the moderns, as follows:

"I have read numerous instances of humanity in the moderns, but none has ever excited my admiration, or affected me more, than one which I lately met with of Sir Philip Sidney. This amiable and truly gallant man, at the battle near Zutphen, fought with the most distinguished bravery. He was twice dismounted, by having his horse killed under him; but, whilst remounting a third, a musket shot, discharged from the trenches, wounded and broke the bone of his thigh. With difficulty he rode to the camp, which was at the distance of a mile and a half. Exhausted, almost to fainting, with loss of blood, and parched with thirst, the weather being

extremely warm, he entreated something
might be given him to drink. This was instantly brought him: he seized it with eagerness; but, at the moment he was carrying the
cooling draught to his mouth, he saw a poor
wounded soldier borne along, who cast a
wishful look at it. The generous Sidney
forgot his own sufferings in those of the
object before him, and taking the bottle
from his mouth, untasted, presented it to the
wounded soldier, compassionately saying,
'Thy necessity is yet greater than mine.'"

"I can never," said Edmund, "hear or read
of Sir Philip Sidney, but I think of our brave
Sir Sidney Smith; and I always imagine there
is a great similarity in their dispositions and
characters. They both seem to me to possess the same spirit of gallantry and humanity."

"Your observation has a great deal of
truth in it, Edmund," replied Sir Hubert,
"and gives me a pleasing conviction, that
you are not always so hasty in your judgment
as you lately accused yourself of being. One
of the best methods of improving the mind,
and exercising the memory, is this, of accus-
toming yourself to draw a parallel between

great characters; and, at the same time, nothing more embellishes conversation."

" This story of Emily's," said Jane, " re-
calls to my mind a similar instance of humanity and self-denial, which I will, as well as I
can remember, tell you."

" Our great and good King Alfred, after
being, with his army, defeated by the Danes,
retreated to a small castle, which he possessed
in the island of Athelney, in Somersetshire.
While he was there, he was one day accosted
by a poor beggar, who implored him to relieve his distress.—' We have,' said the queen,
' but one loaf left for ourselves and our
friends, who are gone out in search of food,
but with very little hope of success.'—The
king replied, ' Give the poor Christian one
half of the loaf. He that could feed five
thousand men with five loaves and two fishes,
can make that half of the loaf sufficient for
our necessities. This noble act of humanity
was speedily rewarded by that Providence, on
whom, in all his troubles, this amiable monarch put his trust. His friends returned
successful from their search for provisions,
and brought sufficient to relieve and support

H

them for a considerable time longer, till they
obtained other supplies."

"What a dreadful thing it must be," said
Charles, "for a queen to be reduced to such
distress. One cannot help being more affected by the sufferings of women than of
men; and when a woman has been bred in
all the indulgences and splendour of a throne,
and is suddenly reduced from it, they must
possess a hard heart indeed, who are not in-
terested in their sufferings."

"Your remark," said Lady Arborfield,
"my good boy, convinces us that you possess,
in no small degree, the virtue we are expati-
ating on; and I hope that, as you are amply
blessed with the power of indulging it, your
natural impulse may never be checked by instances you may meet with of imposture or
ingratitude. But I must now tell you my
story; and I am glad to say, that it respects a
very worthy gentleman, now living."

"Mr. Dale, an eminent merchant of Glasgow, is as remarkable for his philanthropy as
for his public spirit. He built a village, and
established a manufactory, which employed
and supported more than fifteen hundred

poor people; a service of the greatest importance in Scotland, where, in consequence of a
great number of farms being thrown into one,
and all converted into sheep-walks, the poor
people have lost all means of supporting
themselves by labour; and are therefore obliged, by thousands, to leave their country, or
starve. But the good are often afflicted with
calamity. In one night, by some accident,
the manufactory took fire, and the whole of
the building, with all its complicated ma-
chinery and expensive apparatus, was reduced
to ashes.

" The next morning a crowd of young
people assembled round the smoking ruins:
when they beheld the destruction of all they
depended on for support, and thought on the
miserable condition to which they were reduced, their hearts were too full to speak, but
they suddenly, one and all, burst into tears.

" The worthy master of these weeping
children beheld their grief with pity: regardless of his own immense loss, and anxious
only to sooth their sorrows, he thus addressed them: 'My good children, do not cry;
your situation is better than it was before;
for, till the manufactory is rebuilt, you will
have nothing to do but play, and shall still

receive the same wages.' And this generous
promise was followed by actual performance."

"How generous! how humane!" exclaimed the whole party.

"You talk of going to the Lakes next
summer, my dear papa," said Edmund, "pray
do let us go on to Glasgow, when we are
there; I should so love to see this good Mr.
Dale."

"Your generous enthusiasm shall certainly be indulged," replied the worthy baronet,
taking the spirited boy affectionately by the
hand; "and, I confess, I shall myself receive
much gratification in becoming acquainted
with this worthy philanthropist; at the same
time, we shall all be amused as well as instructed, by inspecting the ingenious ma-
chinery by which so many children are enabled to obtain their own livelihood. You
side with the moderns," continued he, turning to George; "I conclude you have strong
reasons for deserting us. What illustrious
hero, or heroine, is to be the subject of your
panegyric?"

"A heroine illustrious only by her virtue,"
answered George; "a poor servant girl of the
city of Noyon, in France."

" A common sewer, of considerable depth, had been opened at Noyon, for the purpose of repair; four men passing by, late in the evening, unfortunately fell in, no precautions having been taken to prevent so probable an accident.

" It was midnight before their situation was known; and, of course, at such an hour it was not easy to procure assistance. However, at length some few people were collected together; but every person who came was afraid to attempt the rescue of the poor men,, for fear of sharing their fate. Thus they would have been left to perish, had it not been for the benevolent intrepidity of Catha-rine Vassent, a poor servant girl, not more than seventeen years old. Fearless of danger, and melted by the tears and cries of their wives and children, she pressed through the crowd; and, having fastened a cord round her body, she desired to be let down into the frightful chasm. When she reached the bottom, she found the poor men almost suffocated; she instantly fixed the cord securely round two of them, and they were drawn up, by those above, and happily restored to life. While thus nobly employed, her breath began to fail; and she had scarcely fastened the cord to the body of a third man, when she found herself on the point of fainting; she had, however, presence of mind sufficient to fix the rope firmly to her own hair, which hung in long and luxuriant tresses.

"The people above, though they felt no inclination to imitate her humane heroism, willingly contributed such assistance as they could afford, with safety to themselves; and, on pulling up what they supposed to be the bodies of the other men, they saw, with surprise and concern, the generous Catharine suspended by her hair, swinging on the same cord, apparently lifeless. Fresh air, with proper remedies, soon restored this heroic girl; and she had the fortitude to descend again into the pestilential opening, in the hopes of saving the unfortunate man who remained; but, in consequence of the delay produced by her indisposition, he was drawn up an irrecoverable corpse.

"Her conduct did not pass unnoticed: a procession of the corporation and a solemn Te Deum took place on the occasion. Catharine received the public thanks of the Duke of Orleans, the Bishop of Noyon, and the town magistrates. A medal, commemorating her glorious intrepidity, with considerable pecu-

niary rewards and a civic crown, were also
bestowed on her; but she found a reward,
greater than all these, in beholding the happiness of those families, who, but for her,
would have been hapless widows and orphans;
and the congratulations of her own heart
were the best recompence of all."

"What a noble girl," cried Emily.

"What infamous cowards," cried Edmund, "must all the rest have been, to have
suffered her to descend again into this dangerous place, after it had so nearly proved
fatal to her. I protest they deserved to have
been thrown in themselves, and to have had
no one but such as themselves behold their
fate."

"That is almost too uncharitable an idea,"
said his mother; "and yet I do not know, in
what terms to express sufficiently the contempt, which the selfish insensibility of these
people deserved. I believe we must follow the
example of those who rewarded poor Catharine, and express our sense of her generous humanity, by assigning her the first rank among
those whom we have celebrated to-night."

"Hold!" cried Sir Hubert, "not quite so
fast: let us first discuss the merits of the rest.

And, in the first place, what have you to say to my good bishop of Amida?"

"We have already expressed our opinion," said Lady Arborfield, of his benevolence and goodness. He did honour to his sacred office; and, while he evinced the goodness of his own heart, he gave a striking proof of the purity and simplicity of that religion, of which he was so worthy a minister, when he showed, that the God he worshipped delighted more in the happiness of his creatures, than in splendid sacrifices to himself; and was better pleased with the offerings of an humble heart, than with all the pomp of ceremony. But, without detracting from his merits, on the score of humanity, it must be observed, that this religion, with which his mind was so strongly impressed, enjoined such acts as a duty; and he would, therefore, have thought himself offending against religion, as well as morality, if he had done otherwise than he did."

"At all events, then," said Charles, "the good bishop did well; for few people are found who always perform their duty."

"Even this objection," said Edmund, "cannot be urged against Metellus, for I do not re-collect that the religion of the Romans taught

them to give up what was advantageous to
themselves, for the sake of humanity to others;
and they certainly were instructed, in all the
contests with their enemies, to spare neither
others, nor themselves: and, as my father observed, had he been unsuccessful in his expedition, this mercy would have been alleged
against him as a crime, and, as the cause of
his ill success; and he would have been stripped of his honours, and sent into banishment.
When we think of all this, I do not know how
you can well point out a greater instance of
humanity than this of Metellus."

"I quite agree with you, Edmund," answered Charles, "that, considering every thing,
this action of Metellus was very noble and humane; but I will not say, that I conceive it
impossible to be excelled. A man is scarcely
entitled to praise, because he does not do all
the harm in his power; I do not mean to infer,
however, that this is precisely the case with
Metellus, because he raised the siege, rather
than injure these innocent victims, and resigned a certain advantage to himself, rather than
obtain it by the sacrifice of humanity. It
might, it is true, be said, in answer to this,
that the place, perhaps, was not of so much
importance, as to influence the success of the

whole expedition; and, that he knew human nature so well, as to be aware that this lenity would conquer more than his arms."

"That would be scrutinizing the motives of human actions too severely," observed Sir Hubert, "and resolving every thing into self-interest. I did not know you were so nice a casuist; I am afraid that few of us could bear the test of such severe criticism."

"I did not mean, my dear uncle," replied Charles, "to say, that this was my own opinion of Metellus, I merely intended to show my cousin, that it was not impossible, but that there might be actions still more disinterested, than this of the Roman proconsul. At the same time, I entreat you to believe, that I do not wish to insinuate, that the conduct of Antigonus has a superior claim to admiration; and, I wish Edmund to be as free in his remarks upon him, as I have been upon his hero."

"You are very liberal my dear Charles," said Edmund, "but I really cannot find any thing in the conduct of Antigonus, but what is worthy of praise. The generous pity, which he expressed for the fate of the treacherous Pyrrhus, who sought his ruin by every means in his power, fills me with love and admiration; and his humane attention to the son of this rival, was more glorious to him than his victory."

"I am extremely obliged to you," answered Charles, "for having pleaded the cause of my hero, so much better than I could have done myself."

"These were very great and noble men, to be sure," said Emily; "but, I think I may venture to place our gallant Sir Philip Sidney in competition with them, without fear of his lustre being diminished by the comparison."

"Well, really," cried Edmund, "though I admire the character of Sir Philip Sidney, and think him an honour to the English nation, I do not see, in this action, any thing so wonderful. It was, certainly, very good-natured, to give the poor soldier what he wanted himself, but it was only a little water."

"It was only a little water!" replied George; "but that little water was then more valuable to him, than all the wealth or power in the world. He was parched up with heat, and thirst, and feverish from his wounds: his eyes were tantalized with the cooling draught; and yet he resigned it to another, because he saw him languish for it. All, who have been shipwrecked, have wandered in the wilds of

Africa, have been confined in dungeons, or
have otherwise been reduced to famine, have
described the sensation of thirst, as exceeding
all other agonies that can be imagined, or endured. You must not, therefore, think it a
trifling sacrifice, which the gallant Sir Philip
made, nor consider it less entitled to admiration, because others, in the same circumstances, have acted in the same manner."

"All that can be said for our good king Alfred and his queen, has already been said by
my cousin George, in defending the merits of
Sir Philip Sidney. But I must confess," continued Jane, "that I do not think the action
of the king equal, in point of humanity and
self-denial, to that of the gallant knight; because, though his distress was very great, yet
it evidently was not so pressing, or immediate."

"I am aware," said Lady Arborfield, "that
with you, who make such nice and severe dis-
criminations between the different shades of
virtue, my Scotch merchant will not rank in
the first scale of philanthropists. Edmund
thinks money nothing; and yet, you will allow
that a man must have no small share of kindness for his fellow-creatures, in his nature,
when he could suppress his feeling for his own

misfortunes, to exert himself to alleviate the distress of others."

"As you related the story, my dear aunt," said Charles, "I observed you mentioned that Mr. Dale told the poor children, they would be better off than they were before, because they would have nothing to do but to play till the manufactory was rebuilt. Was this perfectly right to teach poor children to consider labour a task, which it was desirable to be relieved from?"

"Your question is judicious," replied the good lady; "but we must remember, that the worthy merchant said this in the overflowing of his heart, and was not then so anxious to instruct, as to console them. I believe, however, I was right in my first opinion, that the crown of merit must be given to Catharine Vassent."

"I really think so too," said Emily; "and I willingly resign the pretensions of the brave Sir Philip to the superior claims of this French peasant girl."

"And I those of Metellus," said Edmund. "There was something so noble, so incomparable, in her attempting what all others were afraid to hazard; and in descending a second

I

time into the frightful gulph, that had already
nearly deprived her of life."

"You are very kind," said George, "my
good friends, to save me the trouble of expa-
tiating on the virtue of the good Catharine.
But, as my father is our judge, we are taking
the province out of his hands, by deciding
ourselves on the comparative merits of those,
whose actions we have been relating. And
we appeal to you, Sir, therefore, for a confir-
mation of our judgment."

The worthy baronet assented to the reasons that were adduced in Catharine's favour;
and, after a slight repast, the young friends
retired to their respective apartments.

The party at Holly Hall met each other, on the fourth evening since our introduction of them to our young readers, with smiles of cheerful expectation; and having already decided on Friendship as the theme for their present discussion, Charles related the following anecdote, as the noblest instance of it that occurred to his recollection.

"It was after the second memorable battle at Philippi, where Brutus, with his army, experienced a total defeat, that Lucilius, his friend and confidant, gave him a noble proof that he deserved this distinction. Being aware that Brutus was in the greatest danger of falling into the power of his enemies, he determined to avert this misfortune at the risk of his own life. He, therefore, threw himself in the way of a party, who were in search of his unfortunate friend, and, in pursuance of his generous resolution, gave Brutus an opportunity of making his escape, by declaring to the soldiers who were in pursuit of him, that he was himself the object of their search. 'I am Brutus,' said this generous friend; 'lead me to Antony.' These soldiers were a band of Thracians, unacquainted with the person of Brutus, and readily believed the assertion of Lucilius. He was immediately led into the presence of Antony, who was debating with himself in what manner he should receive and treat Brutus, who, he believed, was on the point of being delivered up to him. On the entrance of Lucilius, he instantly discovered the mistake of his soldiers. Lucilius preserved the most undaunted courage in this situation, and discovered no anxiety, but for the preservation and honour of his friend. 'I have taken the name of Brutus,' said he, 'but to preserve him from falling alive into the hands of his enemies. The gods will not permit that fortune should triumph so far over virtue; and should he be taken, either alive or dead, Brutus will be found in a situation worthy of his illustrious character. As for myself, I value my own life only as it has enabled me to preserve one so much more precious to Rome; and yield it with triumph, now I have succeeded.' Antony

could not conceal his admiration of this conduct;
and generously pardoning a deception which
had so disinterested an object in view, expressed, in the warmest terms, his approbation; then
turning to the enraged Thracians, whom Lucilius had deceived, he addressed them in the
following words:—'I perceive, my friends,
that the generous fraud that has been practised on you, has provoked in you the strongest
resentment; but know, if you have failed in
delivering to me the enemy you expected,
yet you have brought me what is a far more
estimable prize—you have brought me a
friend, for such I hope to make him: and is
it not far more honourable to have such a
man as Lucilius for a friend than an enemy?'
Then addressing himself to Lucilius, he said,
'I can offer thee, generous man, no reward
equal to thy merit—Brutus is now dead, and
thy noble friendship has lost its object.—I
restore thee thy liberty, and ask but this in
return, be to Antony what thou hast been to
Brutus; and, if thou canst, love me as thou
didst him.' Lucilius, penetrated with this
noble candour and forbearance, embraced the
interests of Antony, and adhered as firmly to
him as he had to Brutus. He never forsook
him, when he was deserted by every one else."

"How unfortunate it was that Brutus did not live to enjoy longer such a friend as Lucilius!" said Edmund: "I am sure I should have thought such a friend a greater blessing than a thousand conquests."

"So thought Antony," replied Sir Hubert; "and in this instance did himself honour. A generous disposition will never exult over a fallen foe: and Antony knew that, by attaching such a man as Lucilius to his interests, he acquired a treasure, of which no reverse of fortune could deprive him. I will myself relate an anecdote of the Romans, which affords another proof how high a sense they entertained of this exalted virtue, and how ready they were, at all times, to sacrifice themselves in its cause."

"Caius Gracchus, who was the idol of the Roman people, having carried his regard for the plebeians so far as to draw on himself the resentment of the nobility, an open rupture ensued. The consul Opimius, who espoused the cause of the latter, seized a post, which commanded the city. Gracchus and Fulvius, his friend, with a confused multitude, took possession of Mount Aventine; so that the two extremities of Rome, to the east and

the west, were like two camps. Overtures
of peace were made, but not being accepted,
a battle ensued, in which the consul, meeting
with a more vigorous opposition than he expected, proclaimed a pardon for those who
should lay down their arms; and, at the same
time, set a price on the heads of Gracchus
and Fulvius, promising to give their weight
in gold to any one who should bring them to
him.   This proclamation had the desired
effect; the populace slipped away one by one,
and, deserting their leaders, returned silently
to their own houses. Fulvius, by the vigilance of the consular party, was taken and
beheaded. As for Gracchus, he would have
taken refuge in the temple of Diana; but Li-
cinius Crassus, his brother-in-law, and Pomponius, a Roman knight, who attended him,
advised him to make his escape from thence.
He followed their advice, and passing through
the centre of the city, got to the bridge Sub-
licius, where his enemies, who pursued him
close, would have overtaken and seized him,
had not his two friends, with the greatest intrepidity and resolution, opposed their fury;
but they saw the danger he was in, and determined to save his life, even at the expence
of their own. They defended the bridge alone

against all the consular troops, till Gracchus
was out of their reach; and, at length, being
overpowered by numbers, and covered with
wounds, they both expired on the bridge,
which they had immortalized by their glorious exploit. In the meanwhile Gracchus
fled to a sacred wood, dedicated to the Furies,
and there ordered a generous slave, by name
Euphorus, or, as others call him, Philostratus,
who had attended him, to put an end to his
life. The faithful slave, resolving not to out-
live his master, stabbed himself with the same
dagger which he had plunged into the breast
of Gracchus, and expired with him."

"I do not recollect any instance, at present," said Edmund, "of a person sacrificing
his life for his friend; but I have been much
pleased with one, which I will relate to you,
of the confidence with which the sentiment
of friendship inspired a citizen of Corinth, in
the last moments of his life."

"Eudamidas, the person I speak of, was
in very indigent circumstances, and drawing
near his end, his mother and daughter were
threatened with absolute poverty. This did
not appear, however, to give the dying man

any concern; but, on his decease, a circumstance was discovered, which accounted for
this apparent insensibility. He had made a
will, a few hours before he expired, contain-
ing these memorable words: 'I bequeath to
Aretæus the maintenance of my mother, and
her support under old age; and to Charixenes,
I bequeath and appoint the disposal of my
daughter in marriage, and desire him to give
her the best dowry in his power to bestow; and,
in case either of my said two friends should
die, then I substitute the survivor to perform
what the other should have done, had he
lived.' When this testament was read, it excited, at first, the astonishment of those who
heard it; but, considering only the poverty of
Eudamidas, and not knowing his connection
with the legatees, they treated the matter as
a mere pleasantry, and went out laughing at
the legacies bequeathed to them. But not so
those in whose friendship he had placed such
noble confidence. Immediately that they
heard the report of it, they came and hastened
to ratify solemnly the engagements enjoined
them by their departed friend. Charixenes,
however, did not live to execute his part of
the trust, for, in a few days after the death of
Eudamidas, he expired; and, as the will ex-

pressed, the two-fold charge devolved on
Aretæus. This excellent man generously discharged the duty imposed on him. He
adopted the aged mother of Eudamidas, and
treated her with the same filial attention as
the one bestowed on him by nature; and, in
giving the daughter in marriage to an amiable
man, he endowed her with a portion equal to
that of his own daughter, who was married
on the same day."

" Well, I declare," exclaimed Charles,
when Edmund had finished his story, " this is
the strangest will I ever heard of; and I cannot help thinking, that there are few people
now that would have observed it so strictly as
Aretæus did."

" Nay, my dear cousin," said George, " do
not condemn the moderns unheard; I think I
can relate an instance similar, and nothing inferior, to this of Edmund's, and that too of a
modern."

" The author I quote from, Monsieur Se-
daine, has neglected to give the name of the
gentleman, whose enthusiastic friendship has
given me the opportunity of taking up the
cause of the moderns on this subject. But

we understand from him, that he was a man
of rank and fortune; and that he had a friend,
who, at his death, left his affairs in a very de-
ranged state, and two children totally unpro-
vided for. In a short time, the gentleman
was observed to have adopted a very rigid
plan of economy. He put down his equi-
page, quitted his mansion, discharged his servants, all but one footman, and took apartments in a small house; from whence he
walked every day to the palace, followed by
his servant, to discharge the duties of his
post. This conduct did not fail to draw on
him a load of calumny: imprudence, avarice,
and the most unworthy motives were alternately imputed to him; but he nobly disdain-
ed them all; and, at the end of two years, he
reappeared in the world, having accumulated
the sum of twenty thousand pounds. This
he generously applied to the payment of his
deceased friend's debts, and to the service of
his orphans; and thus rescued the memory of
a worthy man from shame, and a helpless offspring from misery and ruin."

"I am happy to find, George," said his
cousin, "that you can so well refute my hasty
assertion. Indeed, I ought not to have made

it; for, as we have decided in favour of the
moderns every night hitherto, I had no reason to suppose, that they were more deficient
in friendship, than in other virtues."

"My brother George," said Emily, "has
produced a modern instance, parallel with that
of the good Corinthian, Aretæus. I am glad
that I can recollect one, that happened almost
within our own time, resembling exactly that
of Lucilius, the generous friend of Brutus.

"Roderick Mackenzie, a young merchant
of Edinburgh, attached himself to the cause
of the Pretender, in the year 1745. He was
about the same age as Prince Charles, and
much resembled him in person. He was not
only attached to him from principles, but was
fascinated by his elegant manners and conde-
scending affability. The prince was equally
struck with the fervent and disinterested attachment of the young merchant, and a firm
and intimate friendship commenced between
them. After the total defeat of Prince Charles,
at Culloden, Mackenzie followed his leader's
fate. They wandered about for some time
among the hills round Glenmoriston, and endured all the hardships which fatigue, hunger,
and dread of discovery could inflict. Stimu-

lated by these, Mackenzie one day imprudent-
ly ventured farther from the place of their
concealment than he had been accustomed to
do while it was light, having before prevailed
on the prince to remain quiet till his return.
Unfortunately he was discovered by some of
the soldiers, who were in pursuit of his leader.
Mackenzie instantly perceived that they had
mistaken him for the object of their pursuit; and
instantly reflecting, how essentially he might
serve his prince, by deceiving his pursuers, he
nobly resolved on preserving the life of his
friend by the sacrifice. He was determined,
however, not to yield himself a tame victim
to his adversaries; he drew his sword, and
fought bravely in defence of his life. His
steadiness and undaunted courage confirmed
the soldiers in their belief of his being the
young Pretender; and, at length, one of them
shot him. The generous Mackenzie fell, ex-
claiming, ' Traitors, you have murdered your
prince!' and he expired, repeating these words.
The soldiers, congratulating each other on the
certainty of having secured to themselves the
reward of thirty thousand pounds, offered by
government for the head of the Pretender, immediately cut off that of Mackenzie, and hastened to claim their reward, by carrying it

K

to Fort Augustus. Mackenzie had not sacrificed his life in vain. Several, who were
supposed to be well acquainted with the person of Prince Charles, declared the head to
be his. This news was soon carried to the
Duke of Cumberland, who, in consequence,
immediately set off for London. The search,
of course, was suspended; and, by this heroic
act of friendship, which he did not hear of
till some time afterwards, Prince Charles was
enabled ultimately to evade his pursuers."

" I cannot help feeling for this unfortunate
prince, in being deprived of the society of the
noble Mackenzie, which must have been such
a consolation to him in his misfortunes; and
the manner in which he lost him," continued
Jane, " must have added the severest poignan-
cy to his grief. I remember reading an anecdote in the History of England, which very
much affected me at the time, that this story
of Emily's reminded me of.

" Henry the Second was of a very generous
and affable disposition, and treated those noblemen of his court, who were eminent for
their virtues, as friends, rather than subjects.
Among this distinguished number was Hu-

bert de St. Clare; on whom, however, the
king does not seem to have bestowed any extraordinary favours, except that of personal
kindness.

"At the siege of Bridgenorth castle, which
was defended by Roger de Mortimer, the king
exposed himself to much danger. While he was
busied in giving orders, near the wall of the
fortress, one of Mortimer's archers aimed an
arrow, which would certainly have killed him.
The generous Hubert, perceiving the danger
of his beloved monarch, the moment that the
archer drew the fatal string, stepped before
the body of his friend, and received the arrow
in his own breast. The wound was mortal;
and the brave Hubert expired in the arms of
his master, recommending his infant daughter
to his protection. Henry, affected beyond
description, by this noble deed, shed tears of
the bitterest regret over the corpse of his
faithful and generous friend. He vowed to
observe, sacredly, his dying request, and called
on Heaven to witness the solemn engagement.
He educated the daughter of his preserver
with the most sedulous attention, and bestowed on her all that affection and gratitude,
which he owed to her lamented father. His
regard and care of her never relaxed; and,

when she arrived at the age of maturity, he bestowed her, as the noblest gift in his possession, on William de Longueville, a nobleman of the greatest distinction, on condition of his taking the name of St. Clare, which the grateful monarch was determined to perpetuate."

"Poor Hubert," said Edmund, "I have often shed tears over his affecting story; and I am sure I could not help doing so, if I were to read it every day; and yet I love to read it too."

"That's my good boy," exclaimed his admiring father; " these are the natural effusions of a warm heart; and, though I would repress in you every tendency to weakness, or enervating sensibility, the genuine feelings of benevolence will ever give me the sincerest delight."

Edmund's expressive eyes beamed with rapture at the applause of his father, and Lady Arborfield proceeded with the amusements of the evening, in the following manner:

"The incident I mean to tell you, my dear children, I fancy will not fail to interest you, as it will show the firm attachments which are sometimes formed at school.

" Lord Stanhope was at Eton school with
one of the Scotch noblemen, who were condemned for having joined the Pretender, in
the rebellion of 1715. He had never seen his
friend since their school days; but his affectionate remembrance was not effaced by so
long a separation. While the privy council
were deliberating upon signing the warrant of
these unfortunate noblemen, he requested them
to spare the life of his friend. His request
was refused; with which he was so much
grieved and offended, that he declared his intention of resigning his place. This menace
he persisted in, and at length it had the desired effect. The privy council yielded to his
threats, what they had refused to his entreaties
He instantly communicated the pleasing in-
telligence to his associate in early life, and, at
the same time, conveyed him a handsome sum
of money, to assist him in his exile."

" We have produced so many instances so
nearly alike," said Sir Hubert, " that I am
afraid we shall have considerable difficulty in
making any distinction of merit between them.
But our friend Charles is such an able casuist
that I conclude he will find reasons for giving
the friend of Brutus the preference."

"It is impossible for me," answered Charles, " to say any thing more in favour of Lucilius, than barely to relate the story; the action speaks sufficiently for itself; nor do I think there is a single point of his conduct open to attack or suspicion."

" Not as a friend, perhaps, my dear cousin," said George; " but his principles do not seem to have been very firmly fixed, or he never would have accepted the friendship, and sided with the party, of the debauched tyrant Antony, after having been so intimately connected with the virtuous republican Brutus."

"Come, come," said Sir Hubert, " even you, George, are here straying from the point in question. We do not speak of the political principles or attachments of Lucilius, but of his attachment to his friend; and, in this respect, it cannot be denied, that his conduct was most disinterested and noble."

" The action of Roderick Mackenzie," said Emily, "resembles, as I said before, that of Lucilius so exactly, that I can perceive scarcely any difference between them ; and I cannot suggest any reason for claiming the superiority for Mackenzie, unless we may conclude, from his chusing to die in the defence of his friend, that no circumstances could have in-duced him to become the friend of his enemies; as Lucilius did of those who pursued the noble Brutus with the most inveterate hatred."

"I am going to do," said Sir Hubert, "what I have just checked in George; but I cannot avoid observing, that, while we admire and praise the virtue of young Mackenzie, we must regret that it was not exerted in a better cause. His friend was a proscribed alien, seeking to overturn the constitution of his country, and, by joining himself to him, therefore, Mackenzie became a traitor to his king. The same objection will apply, however, in some measure, to the friends of Gracchus. This Roman is as much panegyrized by some, as he is virulently abused by others; and though he certainly does not deserve the reproach of the one party, some deduction must be made from the praise that has been lavished upon him by the other. He was a very honest man, and his intentions were good; but, while he sought to increase the liberty of the people, he committed violences against the law of the state, and introduced licentiousness under the name of reform. Whatever, therefore, is the degree of blame that can be attached to Gracchus, his friends are involved in it. Their attachment, however, to him personally is the same; and

we cannot withhold our admiration of the exalted proof which they gave of their friendship and bravery."

"You have not noticed, my dear papa,"
said Emily, "the affection of the poor slave.
If I may be allowed to express my opinion,
I think the attachment which he showed for
his master, is quite as singular as that of his
two noble friends."

"I think so too," added Edmund; "and
is more deserving of notice, as we do not expect, in persons of his condition, such generosity of sentiment: at the same time it
proves what my father said, that Gracchus
must have been a very good and amiable
man, to have inspired his slave with so much
affection and devotion. In the anecdote
which I related of the generous Corinthians,
I do not know which most to admire, the
noble confidence of poor Eudamidas, or the
cheerfulness and benevolence with which his
friends accepted the extraordinary bequest.
I can readily suppose what George will say,
to prove that the claims of his French gentleman are superior to those of Aretæus. He
will say, that he took the charge of his friend's
orphans upon him unasked, and bore the load
of calumny, which his mysterious conduct

occasioned, with patience; and, satisfied with
the purity of his own motives, braved suspi-
cions, which, to an honourable mind, are
worse than death."

" Thank you, thank you," cried George,
laughing. " I protest you have found arguments for me which would not have occurred
to myself; and, by their so readily occurring
to you, I suppose you feel the justice of them
yourself."

" If the sacrifice of life," said Jane, " be
considered the greatest test of friendship,
Hubert de St. Clare is entitled to rank with
Lucilius or Mackénzie, or the friends of
Gracchus. Nor is there the same ground to
detract from his merits. He did not go over
to the enemies of his friends, as Lucilius; nor
was engaged in the cause of rebellion, as
Mackenzie; nor assisted in disturbing the
peace of his country, as the friends of Gracchus; but he gave up his life to preserve his
king, though this life was so valuable to him
on account of his daughter, whom his friendship made an orphan."

" You have really made your hero appear
so amiable," said Lady Arborfield, " that I
am ashamed to bring mine in competition
with him; and, indeed, I ought to observe,

that the conduct of Lord Stanhope was not entirely free from objection, since he made use of his influence to arrest the course of justice, which, though tempered with mercy, should never give way to private interest."

"I confess, said the worthy baronet, "I did not think it would have been so easy a matter to decide this question; but Jane is really, as I before observed, quite a rhetorician; though she speaks so seldom, she always speaks to the purpose; and, as I do not believe we shall be able to refute her arguments, we must consent to give the first place, among illustrious friends, to the gallant Hubert de St. Clare."

"WE have to-night," said Sir Hubert, when our young friends had arranged themselves, "an important subject to discuss. Justice has been said to comprehend every virtue which reason prescribes, or society has a right to expect. Our duty to our Maker, to each other, and to ourselves, is fully performed, if we give to each what in justice we owe. And as to be perfectly just is an attribute of the Divine Nature, so to be just to the utmost of our abilities is the perfection of human nature. The rule cannot be better laid down than it is in the words of the Divine Founder of our religion: 'Do unto others as ye would they should do unto you.' For this golden rule, Alexander Severus, one of the best of the Roman emperors, had such an uncommon veneration, that he ordered it to be engraved, in large capitals, over the gate of his palace, and on the doors of many of the public buildings."

" Aristides was so much distinguished for his integrity, that he received the glorious surname of the Just. Among innumerable instances that are related of him, there is one which proves how highly he merited this virtuous distinction.

" Themistocles, one of the most celebrated Athenian warriors, once declared, in a full assembly of the people, that he had a project to propose of the greatest public utility; but that he could not communicate it to the citizens at large, because the success of it depended greatly on the secrecy which was observed in its execution. He, therefore, requested they would appoint a person, to whom he might explain himself, without any danger of a discovery. Aristides was the person fixed upon, by the whole assembly, to receive the communication; and they had so much confidence in his prudence and honesty, that they referred the matter entirely to his opinion. Themistocles, therefore, having taken him aside, informed him, that the project he had conceived was, to burn the fleet of the Grecian states, their allies, which then lay in the neighbouring port, called the Piræus: adding that, by this means, Athens would become absolute mistress of the sea,

and the umpire of all Greece. After this ex-
planation, Aristides returned to the assembly,
and assured them, that nothing could be more
beneficial to the republic than the project of
Themistocles; but, at the same time, nothing
could be more unjust and dishonourable. On
hearing this, the people unanimously voted,
that Themistocles should desist from his
project."

"What a disgrace," said George, "it was
to Themistocles, to have proposed such a
project. And really I cannot conceive any
title so dignified as that bestowed on Aristides by the Athenians; a title which he so
well deserved, that it is recorded of him, that
although he enjoyed the highest posts in the
government, and had the absolute disposal of
its treasures, he died so poor as not to leave
sufficient to defray his funeral expences. But
the Athenians had so high a sense of his
merit, that they buried him, and afterwards
supported his family in the most honourable
manner. But I am delaying your story,
Charles, which we will now thank you to
relate."

"M. Popilius Læna," said Charles, "the

L

Roman consul, being sent against the Stelliates, a people in Liguria, bordering on the
river Tanarus, killed and took so many prisoners, that, finding the forces of their nation
reduced to ten thousand men, they submitted
to the consul, without settling any terms.
Popilius, regardless of that humanity which
gives a double lustre to conquest, dismantled
their cities, disarmed the inhabitants, and, re-
ducing them all to slavery, sold them, and
all they possessed, to the highest bidder.
But such was the equity of the Roman senate,
that they resented this severe and cruel proceeding; and passed a decree, commanding
Popilius to restore the money he had received
for the sale of the Stelliates, to set them at
liberty, return them their effects, and even
purchase new arms for them; and concluded their decree with words which poste-
rity ought never to forget. 'Victory is glorious, when it is confined to the subduing of
an untractable enemy ; but, it becomes
shameful, when it is made use of to oppress
the unfortunate.'"

"I wish all conquerors, who know so little in what true bravery consists," exclaimed
George, indignantly, " were to receive the

same severe check to their brutal rapacity.
I should have little faith in generals, who behaved so ill in prosperity; for, I should be
fearful that the avarice which could impel
them to such flagrant acts of injustice, would,
if the temptation were offered, induce them
to betray the trust reposed in them."

"Your indignation and severe reflections
on the conduct of Popilius, George," said his
father, "are justifiable; for the wretch, who
can increase the sufferings of a vanquished
foe in so atrocious a manner, may fairly be
suspected of any crime that can disgrace humanity."

"Cambyses, one of the kings of Persia,"
said Edmund, "who was famous for his un-
alterable regard to justice, had a particular
favourite, whom he conceived to be a virtuous
man, and he therefore raised him to the
office of a judge: but the ungrateful wretch,
depending upon the credit he had with his
master, prostituted the honour of his government, and the rights and properties of his
fellow subjects, in such a daring manner, that
causes were bought and sold in the courts of
judicature, as openly as provisions in the
market. Avarice was the ruling passion of

his soul; and those who would gratify it with
the richest oblations, were always certain of
gaining their suit. When Cambyses was informed of this, he was so much exasperated,
that he not only ordered him to be seized and
publicly degraded, but commanded, that his
skin should be stripped over his ears, and the
seat of judgment be covered with it, as a
warning to others. To convince the world
that he was influenced to commit this extraordinary act of severity by no other motive
than the love of justice, he afterwards appointed the son to succeed to the office of his
father."

" But I am sure," said Emily, " if I had
been the son, I should have declined the honour of this distinction; for, how could he
possibly be collected enough to administer
justice, when he could not take his seat, on
these occasions, without being reminded of
the melancholy, though deserved, fate of his
father."

" That, Emily, is not accounted for," said
Edmund; "and, as it does not immediately relate to our subject, we must be content
to remain in ignorance of the manner in

which the new judge reconciled this to his feelings."

"Our immortal bard, Shakespeare, has taken the subject of one of his most beautiful and highly-finished scenes," said George, "from the following circumstance."

"The celebrated Brutus, of whom we spoke last night, upon the accusation of the inhabitants of Sardis, publicly condemned, and branded with infamy, Lucius Pella, who had formerly been censor, and whom Brutus had himself often employed in offices of great confidence; his crime was the having abused the trust reposed in him, by embezzling the public money. Cassius, the friend and half-brother of Brutus, was much offended with him for this sentence; as he conceived it an indirect reproach of his own conduct for having, but a few days before, publicly absolved two of his own friends, and continued them in their offices; and, although they had been accused of the same crimes as Lucius Pella, merely giving them a slight reproof in private. Cassius was of too choleric a disposition to be able to conceal from Brutus how much he was hurt at the difference of his conduct; and he therefore accused him, but

in a friendly manner, of too much austerity
and rigour, where gentleness and kindness
were necessary, and would not fail to prove
of more service to their cause. In answer to
this remonstrance, Brutus reminded him of
the Ides of March, on which day they had
put Cæsar to death; who, though he himself
never oppressed or vexed mankind, instead
of punishing, was the support of those that
did, and thus drew the public odium on himself. He desired Cassius to consider, that if
justice could be neglected, under any false
colouring, for what had they sacrificed Cæsar;
and that it certainly would have been better
to have suffered the injustice of Cæsar's
friends, than to suffer that of their own to remain unpunished. 'For then,' said he, 'we
could have been accused of cowardice only;
whereas now, if we connive at the injustice of
others, we make ourselves liable to the same
accusation, and share with them in the guilt.'
Plutarch, in whom," said George, " I read
this anecdote, remarks, 'That from this we
may judge what was the rule of all the actions
of Brutus.' "

" I love," said Jane, " to read Plutarch's
Lives; he seems to have been so very good-

natured a man, and to have painted every thing in such amiable colours. And this is what we so seldom meet with in biographers, or historians, that it is the more conspicuous in him."

"Very true," said her aunt, "and for this reason; there are few historians, who do not suffer party zeal to bias their relations of facts, and it is from these prejudices, that we find the same actions represented in such different lights."

"I have been highly diverted," said Emily, "with an anecdote that I read a short time since; which, though rather ludicrous, shows how very impartial our good and learned Sir Thomas More was, in his administration of justice.

"There was a poor woman, who had lost a little dog, of which she was very fond: in her enquiries after it, she was informed, that the lady of Sir Thomas More had, in her possession, a dog, which she had lately received as a present; and, from the description, the woman had reason to suppose it to be her own. She, therefore, went immediately to Sir Thomas, as he was sitting in the hall of justice; and complained to him, that his lady withheld her dog from her; Sir Thomas gave orders, that his lady should be directly summoned to appear before him; and, that the dog should be brought with her. When the lady and the dog came, he took the little fellow in his hands, and desired his lady to take her stand at one end of the hall, and the poor woman at the other; and, saying, 'That he sat there to do every one justice,' he placed the dog in the middle of the hall between them, and bid each of them call him; which they no sooner did, than the little dog ran to the poor woman, wagging his tail and fawning upon her, as if glad to see an old acquaintance. Upon this evidence, Sir Thomas said he was convinced that the dog was not his lady's, and therefore bid her go home contented. But my lady was so much pleased with the little animal, that she could not help repining at being deprived of it. She, therefore, offered the poor woman a price for it, which was gladly accepted, and so all parties were satisfied. All the spectators, however, smiled at the manner in which Sir Thomas had enquired out the truth."

"This, I suppose," said Edmund, "is what they call, in law, strong presumptive proof, papa?"

"It is rather, I think, strong circumstancial proof; and it is evident that Sir Thomas thought so, as there can be no doubt, that if any stronger had been required, it could easily have been procured. You have really, my dear Emily," said Sir Hubert, "communicated your own mirthful sensations to us; and, I do not think it possible to refrain from laughing, when we reflect on this curious and singular spectacle in a hall of justice."

The young party having enjoyed this scene in imagination a few minutes, Jane thus resumed the discourse.

"One of the loose favourites of the Prince of Wales, afterwards Henry the Fifth, being arraigned for felony, the prince determined to be present at the trial; hoping to overawe, by his presence, the stern independence of Sir William Gascoigne, who was the judge. But in this attempt he failed; for that just man, unmoved by hope and unawed by fear, not only performed his duty, by passing sentence on the culprit, but ordered the prince himself into custody, for having assaulted, and struck him on the seat of justice.

"The prince, who saw his error the moment he had committed the offence, acted with

a greatness of mind, which astonished every
one, when they considered the dissoluteness
of his life, the strength of his passions, and the
weakness with which he had hitherto resisted
them.   Submitting, without a murmur, to the
orders of that court, which he had so grossly
offended, he followed the officer, who had him
in custody, quietly to prison.   His father,
Henry the Fourth, on being informed of the
whole circumstance, exclaimed, in a transport
of joy, ' Happy is the king, who has a magistrate that has courage to execute the laws;
and still more happy, in having a son, who
will submit to their chastisement!' The prince
himself, on ascending the throne, after the
death of his father, sent for Sir William Gascoigne; and, applauding him for his past conduct, warmly exhorted him to persevere in the
same strict and impartial execution of the
laws."

"This was the glorious prince," said George,
" who was afterwards the pride of England,
and the scourge of France; but I do not
know whether he is more to be admired as a
conqueror, in the field of Agincourt, or as a
prisoner, in the court of justice."

This observation being generally assented

to by the rest of the party, Lady Arborfield, whose story only remained to be told, thus began:

"Khalil Pacha was appointed beglerbeg, or governor of Egypt, in the year 1631. He was a very good and virtuous man, and was much beloved by the people, who had been long accustomed to the tyranny and oppressions of the governors, who had preceded him; for these men, who were chiefly minions of the Ottoman court, preferred, in almost every instance, their own interests, and the gratification of their own passions, to the dictates of justice. All manner of abuses had grown up under their government, and every sort of injustice was committed with impunity. The virtuous Khalil saw this, and was determined upon a reform.

"A Jew, named Yacoub, had for fifteen years exercised, in Cairo, the office of sariaf-baschi, or president of the merchant brokers. All the places and offices of the city were in his hands, and the people groaned under the pressure of his odious vexations; but, as he had always cultivated the favour of the beglerbegs, he had hitherto proceeded, without interruption, in his career of tyranny, Khalil resolved to punish this great criminal. Neither his offered presents, nor the solicitations of the great, could effect a change in his resolution; though the great, who protected him, were more earnest in their solicitations, because the Jew owed them large sums of money, which they feared to lose by his condemnation. When Khalil was informed, that this was the reason of the concern they took in the fate of Yacoub, unwilling that any should suffer by his love of justice, he paid them, out of his own private property, what the Jew owed them, and put him to death.

" When this virtuous man quitted his government, in the spring of 1633, all the merchants shut up their shops, from the first of April, to the end of that month; no beglerbeg had ever before received so flattering a testimony of gratitude from the citizens. Under his government, none had been punished with death, but after a judicial enquiry; a mode of proceeding not often attended to by the despots under the Turkish government.

" Three robbers being one day brought before him, who had just been taken, he ordered them to be tried; one of the officers of the divan represented to him, that all affairs of this kind were not to be subjected to the

strict rules of proceeding; and that it would
be eligible to make use of his authority, and
sentence the rogues to death, without further
enquiry. The pacha, without making any
answer, directed the secretary of the divan to
draw up an order, to demolish the house of
the officer, who had given this advice; and,
having signed it, he charged some of his attendants to put it instantly into execution.
The officer, surprised and alarmed at such
a strange order, approached the pacha, and
humbly entreated to know the motive of his
command. 'How!' exclaimed Khalil, 'does
the destruction of that house, which thou hast
built, affect thee, and shall not God be offended,
if the work of his own hands should be destroyed?' The officer, confounded at the justice of this rebuke, kissed the lower end of
the pacha's robe, and loaded him with bless-
ings; Khalil revoked the order he had given,
and, at the same time, finding the charge
against the robbers to be of no serious nature,
set them all three at liberty; and, such was
the good effect of this well-timed lenity, that,
from that period, the greatest security reigned
throughout the city.

"As the fate of so virtuous a man cannot
fail to interest, I cannot conclude, without in-

M

forming you, that, on his return from his government to Constantinople, the sultan con-
fiscated his whole fortune, and banished him
to the island of Cyprus, with two slaves only.
So true is the old observation, that envy follows merit as its shade. But the virtues of
Khalil soared above the malice of his enemies;
the sultan, soon convinced of his innocence
and honour, restored him to his favour, returned him his whole fortune, and promoted
him to the government of Romania."

"My aunt's observation," said Charles, "on
the envy which pursued the good Khalil, re-
minds me of the anecdote of a man of Athens,
who hated the good Aristides, (with whose
story Sir Hubert began the evening) only because of his virtues. This fellow, who was a
peasant, and unacquainted with the person of
Aristides, when the Athenians were passing
sentence of banishment on him, by ostracism,
asked Aristides to write on the shell, his vote
of banishment. 'Has he done you any wrong,'
said Aristides, 'that you are for punishing
him in this manner?'—'No:' replied the
countryman, 'I do not even know him; but I
am sick of hearing every one call him THE
JUST.' Both in the instance which I adduced,

as well as in that of my uncle's, what appears
to me to be particularly admirable, is, that
the act of justice, so eminent in each, was
that of a whole assembly of men; but I do not
know which is entitled to the greatest degree
of praise."

"I think I can perceive some difference
between them," replied Edmund; "but I do
not know what effect it may have in influen-
cing our judgment respecting them. The
Athenians, in rejecting the proposal of Themistocles, declined what would have been an
advantage to the whole state, but would have
involved the whole state in one common disgrace and abhorrence. The Romans, in re-
senting the conduct of their chief magistrate,
did not resign an advantage to the state, but
only stripped an individual, Popilius, of the
plunder he had so unjustly obtained; and
made friends of enemies, by restoring them
their possessions."

"It must, however, be observed, on the
other hand," said George, "that the advantage declined by the Athenians, was one which
they could not obtain, without injustice to
those who were then their friends and allies,
and had confided themselves to their honour;
while the Romans refused to take advantage

of enemies, whom they had defeated, and who had been compelled to surrender at discretion."

"You argue this point nicely," said Sir Hubert; "but I do not think it likely we shall come to a decision on the subject; the cases seem to be very nearly balanced. Let us hear, Edmund, what you can say for the justice of King Cambyses; or rather, how will you palliate the sanguinary mode which he adopted, to warn others against committing injustice?"

"I do not think it was a very humane one, indeed," replied the boy; "and I can only excuse it by the practice of our own nation, and our own times, which are said to be very refined: I mean, the barbarous custom of hanging criminals in chains; which only serves to shock and disgust the good and humane passenger, without at all answering the purpose for which they are professed to be put there; a striking proof of which, we have in the inhuman murder of Mr. Steel, on Hounslowheath, almost under the gibbet where two men were hanging in chains, so close to the road, that you could almost see, as you passed, their bones staring through the flesh, that was half devoured by birds."

"This is a custom shocking to humanity,"

said Lady Arborfield, "and I wish it were abolished entirely. But the particular instance, you allude to, Edmund, has, I understand, been lately very properly removed."

"What I mentioned of Brutus," said George, "I did for the sake rather of doing credit to his general conduct, than of instancing it as a remarkable, or singular act of justice; for I have a great love and veneration for his character, and am fond of illustrating it. I do not put it, therefore, in competition with the other examples, which you have brought forward."

"Though I related it as rather a laughable story," said Emily, "I would not have you think lightly of Sir Thomas More and his little dog; for, if he would condescend to such a careful examination in trifles, to determine with justice; we must suppose he would act with the same impartiality, on occasions of greater importance."

"In all those acts of justice, which I have heard this evening," said Jane, "I do not remember, that the persons, who performed them, had any thing to fear in so doing; but it was not so with Sir William Gascoigne. To show the impartiality of his administration of justice, and to avenge the violation of the law in his person, he sent the first subject in the kingdom to prison. By this act, he not only exposed himself to the resentment of the king, who might have conceived himself insulted in the person of his son, but to the future revenge of the prince, when he should ascend the throne. But his love of justice outweighed all regard for himself; and he fortunately found in the king and the prince, minds as noble and generous as his own."

"If I may be allowed to undertake the panegyric of Khalil Pacha," said Edmund, "his merit appears to me more conspicuous, as he was alone virtuous among the depraved."

"This is saying rather too much," replied George; "it would be uncharitable to suppose, that there were no other virtuous men in the dominions of the grand sultan. The beglerbegs, indeed, who had preceded him in the government of Egypt, seem to have sold injustice and impunity to crime; and his merit, therefore, was great, in stemming the torrent of corruption that had been introduced. His paying those who suffered losses by the execution of the Jew, showed that he really loved justice, and that money, at least, could not bribe him to deviate from it: and the method he took to convince the officer of the injustice of punishment without trial, evinced at once his ingenuity, his equity, and his piety."

"I feel more difficulty in deciding this question," said Sir Hubert, "than I have in any other on which we have commented; and this arises from the very nature of the subject; for where any two actions are perfectly just, they must be equally so. We may, however, in this decision, be allowed to take other circumstances into consideration. The first two instances, as the public acts of states, we will not compare with those of individuals; and of the others, the two last are certainly most deserving of praise. Their respective merits have been pretty clearly pointed out by Jane and George; and, without national prejudice, for the reasons which Jane has alleged, I believe I may venture to say, that this act of Sir William Gascoigne's is the noblest monument of justice upon record."

TEMPERANCE was the theme of this evening, and, without any prelude, Charles Woodley commenced the subject with the following
story:

"Alexander the Great, having restored
Ada, the sister of Mausolus, king of Caria, to
the throne of her ancestors, the princess resolved to show her gratitude to so generous a
conqueror. For this purpose, having provided a variety of dainties, which had been
improved by all the refinements of Asiatic
luxury, she sent them as a present to the
king, together with the cooks employed in
making them. But the young monarch, who
had no taste for such effeminate delicacies,
thanking her very politely for her kind intentions, sent her word, that he had no occasion
for the cooks; because he had already two very
excellent ones, who had been recommended
to him by his tutor, Leonidas: "A long

march in the morning, to give him a relish for his dinner; and a moderate dinner to create in him an appetite for supper." He added, that Leonidas had always used to search his clothes and chests, when he was a boy, lest his mother, Olympias, from a false indulgence, should have concealed any niceties that might have vitiated and debauched his appetite. This manly temperance and moderation, to which he had been accustomed in his earliest youth, he retained a long time afterwards; for, in his Asiatic expedition, when any scarce fruit, or fish, or any other kind of delicacies, were brought to him, he generally distributed them among his friends, reserving hardly a taste for himself."

" I could not help laughing, Charles," cried Edmund, " when you mentioned that Leonidas used to suspect the mother of Alexander of sending her son dainties. Does it not remind you of the boy at our school, whose mother always sent a servant, two or three times a week, to him, with game and poultry, and all sorts of confectionary? I am sure I shall not very soon forget the passions he threw himself into one day, when the servant,

by some mischance, did not arrive so soon as
he expected."

"Indeed," said George, "I have often
thought I would sooner have eaten the coarsest
fare in the world, than have endured the
ridicule which he met with from the whole
school, for this disgusting anxiety about his
appetite.   I do not know," continued he,
"any character of whom so many instances
of temperance are recorded as Cyrus the
Great; and I should be happy in relating
them, for the amusement of Jane and Emily,
who have not the opportunity of reading
them in the original as we have, if I were not
fearful of engrossing too much of the evening."

The whole party declaring they should be
much amused by the recital; he thus began :

"Cyrus, according to the manners of the
Persians, was, from his infancy, accustomed
to sobriety and temperance, of which he was
a most illustrious example through the whole
course of his life.

"When he was twelve years old, his mother, Mandane, took him with her into Media,
to his grandfather, Astyages; who, from the

many things he had heard in his favour, had
a great desire to see him.   In this court
young Cyrus found very different manners
from those of his own country.   Pride, luxury, and magnificence reigned here universally; but this general corruption had no
effect upon the prince, who continued to live
as he had been brought up, and adhered very
strictly to the principles he had imbibed from
his childhood.   He charmed his grandfather
by his sprightliness and wit; and gained the
affection of the whole court by his noble and
engaging behaviour.

     "Astyages, to render this visit the more
agreeable to his grandson, provided a sump-
tuous entertainment, in which there was the
greatest plenty, and profusion of every thing
that was nice and delicate.   All this variety
of exquisite cheer Cyrus beheld with the
greatest indifference; and even ventured to
remark upon it, with a kind of pleasantry,
which did honour to his understanding, and
gave offence to no one.   'Sir,' said he to his
grandfather, 'if you taste all the dainties now
before you, and reach out your hand to every
dish upon the table, you must take more
trouble for one supper than would be sufficient for a hundred.'—'What!' replied Asty-

ages, 'and is not this, think you, a much
better entertainment than any you have been
used to in Persia?'—' No, indeed!' answered
the prince with a smile; for, in Persia, we
have a much readier and shorter method to
satisfy our hunger; a piece of meat and a
slice of bread do the business at once. But
here, after travelling from this dish to that,
and performing a tedious hunt from one end
of the table to the other, you scarcely at last
obtain your object, which we, Persians, arrive
at with the least trouble in the world.'

"Sacas, the cup-bearer of Astyages, had likewise the office of introducing those persons to
the king, who were permitted to have an audience; but not granting this liberty to Cyrus
as often as he desired it, he had the misfortune to displease the prince; who, therefore,
took every opportunity to mortify him. This
being observed by Astyages, he endeavoured
to remove the dislike of the prince, by commending Sacas for the remarkable neatness
and dexterity with which he performed his
office. 'Is that all, Sir?' replied Cyrus; ' if
such a trifling accomplishment is sufficient to
merit your favour, you shall soon see how
well I am able to deserve it; for, with your
permission, I will immediately take upon me

to serve you much better than he.' Cyrus
accordingly equipped himself like a cup-
bearer, and advancing carefully, with a serious
countenance, a napkin upon his arm, and
holding the cup very neatly upon three of his
fingers, (as was the custom of the ancients,)
he presented it to the king with such a re-
spectful gravity, that neither Astyages nor
his mother, Mandane, could forbear smiling.
Concluding from this that he had performed
his part to their satisfaction, he instantly
threw himself upon his grandfather's neck,
and caressing him very fondly, ' O, Sacas!'
cried he: ' poor, unfortunate Sacas! you are
certainly undone; and I shall have the honour of serving my grandfather instead of
you.' — ' Indeed,' said Astyages, who was
much pleased with the affectionate caresses
of his grandson, ' I must do you the justice to
acknowledge, that you have performed your
part to admiration; nobody can serve with a
better grace; but you forgot one material
ceremony, which is that of tasting.' For
the cup-bearer, it seems, always poured some
of the liquor into his left hand, and tasted it,
before he presented it to the king. ' No,
Sir,' replied Cyrus, ' I did not omit that part
through forgetfulness, but because I suspect-

N

ed there was poison in the liquor.'—'Poison,
child!' exclaimed Astyages, 'how could you
think so?'—'Yes, Sir,' replied the boy, 'I
was afraid of poison; for not long ago, at an
entertainment you gave to your nobles, on
your last birth-day, I plainly saw that your
faithful Sacas had mixed some poison in the
liquor. It was impossible for me to think
otherwise; for, when you had drank of it
pretty freely, I took notice that you were all
surprisingly disordered in body and mind.
Those very things, which you forbid us children to do, you did yourselves. You all spoke
together; nor did any one attend to what
was said, even by the person who sat next to
him. You sung the most nonsensical songs
I ever heard; and yet you all swore that they
were the best in the universe. After that,
when any of you rose up to entertain the
company with a dance, you were so far from
being able to keep time, that you could
scarcely keep on your feet. In short, you
yourself seemed to forget that you was a
king, and they that they were subjects.'—
'Very true, child,' said Astyages; 'but have
you never observed the same disorder in your
father?'—'Never, in my life,' replied Cyrus.
'What then? How is it with him when he

drinks?'—'Why, when he has drunk what he chuses, his thirst is quenched, and that is all.'

"Xenophon," said George, "from whom I quote these anecdotes, continues to say, that the invincible valour of the Persians may be justly ascribed to that temperate and hardy life, to which they were accustomed from their infancy. Add to this the influence of example set them by Cyrus, whose ambition it was to surpass all his subjects in regularity, and who was as abstemious and sober in his manner of life, and as much inured to hardship and fatigue as the meanest of his soldiers. What might not be expected from such a body of troops, so formed, and so principled? At the head of this rough and hardy people, he attempted the conquest of the largest empire in the universe, and succeeded to admiration. After he had completed his victory, he exhorted his brave countrymen not to degenerate from their ancient virtue, that they might not obscure the glory they had acquired; but carefully to preserve that simplicity, sobriety, temperance, and love of labour, by which they had obtained it.

"The same illustrious prince having yielded to the entreaties of one of his friends, to take a dinner with him, and being requested

to name the fare he chose, and the place
where the table should be spread, 'It is my
pleasure,' said he to the mortified courtier,
whom he knew to be too luxurious in his
manner of life, 'that you prepare the entertainment on the banks of the river, to supply
us with water to drink; and that a single loaf
of bread be the only dish upon the table.'"

Jane and Emily having thanked George
for the entertainment he had given them,
Edmund was called on for his example, and
obeyed in the following manner:

"When Agesilaus, king of Sparta, was
presented, by the Thasians, with a large
quantity of the most delicate eatables and
costly liquors, he ordered the whole to be
shared among the slaves, who performed the
drudgery of the camps. The Thasians, with
the utmost surprise, enquiring the motive of
his conduct, he nobly replied: 'That it was
beneath the character of men, who valued
themselves for their probity and courage, to
regale on niceties, which could serve no other
purpose but to provoke and corrupt the appetite. Such dainty trifles,' continued he,
' can be relished only by slaves, who aspire

to no greater pleasure than that of eating and drinking; and I have taken the liberty to bestow them accordingly.' For this reason, he would accept of nothing, for the use of himself and his brave countrymen, but some sacks of flour, which accompanied the present."

"As George has been kind enough to amuse us with so many interesting anecdotes of Cyrus," said Sir Hubert, "I shall, as the evening is pretty far advanced, content myself with telling you a very short one."

"It is related of Socrates, that he was so desirous of gaining an entire command over his appetite, that, after exciting the most violent degree of thirst by hard exercise, he never allowed himself to drink till he had thrown away the first pitcher of water he drew; and to this temperance it is ascribed, that, although he was in Athens during the whole continuance of that dreadful plague, which has been so affectingly described by several eminent writers, he never caught the least infection."

"I wonder," cried Edmund, "if the Turks

are strict observers of this virtue.   As they
are afflicted with the plague so continually, I
think they should have this proof of the effect
of temperance written, and placed in their
eating rooms."

"I believe," answered Sir Hubert, "that
the plague, which desolates Turkey, is more
to be ascribed to the filth, which lies in every
part of their cities, and to the narrowness of
their streets; but chiefly to the extensive
marshes and swamps, with which their coast
abounds, producing noxious and pestilential
vapours."

"The virtue of temperance," said Jane,
"was strongly illustrated in the conduct of
one, who was at the same time one of the
most able statesmen, and the most virtuous
and amiable man that ever lived in any age.

"Sully, the celebrated minister of an equally celebrated monarch, Henry the Fourth of
France, kept up the utmost frugality at his
table.   The same moderation prevailed in his
manner of life at Villebon, which he had been
accustomed to in his youth, in the army.   His
table displayed an elegant economy, where
few dishes were served up, and those dressed
in the plainest and most simple manner.   The

courtiers would often rally and reproach him
for his simplicity, which was so opposite to
their own luxurious style of life. On these occasions, he used to reply in the memorable
words of Socrates. ' If the guests are men of
sense and sobriety, there is sufficient for them;
if they are not, I can very well dispense with
their company.'"

" I wish," said Lady Arborfield, " that the
economy and temperance of these two eminent
men were better observed in the present age.
It is, I fear, owing to the spirit of prodigality
and emulation of each other in luxury, beyond
what their circumstances will warrant, that
we hear so frequently of people being reduced from comparative affluence to absolute
want."

" My hero," said Emily, " is the famous
monarch, Charles the Twelfth of Sweden,
who, though, in the early part of his reign, he
gave little promise of becoming the character
he afterwards proved, had the resolution and
forbearance, from the moment he prepared for
war, to renounce, not only the excesses, but
even the most innocent amusements of his
youth. He commenced a life entirely new,

from which he never after varied in the least.
Alexander and Cæsar were his models in every
thing.   He reduced the luxury of his table to
the exactest frugality, and the splendor of his
habiliments to those of the simplest materials.
He likewise resolved to abstain from wine; as
he conceived it stimulated his naturally fiery
disposition.   This forbearance was the more
remarkable and praiseworthy in him, as sobriety was a virtue, till that time, unknown in
the north.   But Charles was determined to be
a pattern of virtue, in his own person, to all
his subjects."

    " I shall," said Lady Arborfield, " conclude
the examples, that have been given on this
subject, from a book, which I lately read, entitled, The Advantages of a Temperate Life.

    " The author of this book was a Venetian
gentleman, of noble extraction, whose name
was Lewis Cornaro.   He tells us, that, from
the foolish and vicious intemperance of his
youth, he had brought on himself a complica-
tion of disorders; and that, from his thirty-
fifth to his fortieth year, he spent his days
and nights in the utmost anxiety and pain;
and that his life was a burden to him.   The

physicians, however, told him, after many
fruitless efforts to restore his health, that it remained with himself to make one more trial,
which, if he could prevail on himself to persevere in, might, in time, free him from all his
complaints. This was to abandon his former
habits, and adopt a temperate and regular
way of living. But they added, that unless
their advice were followed immediately, his
case would soon become desperate. After
many struggles with his former inclinations,
he at last grew confirmed in a settled and
uninterrupted course of temperance; by virtue of which, as he assures us, all his disorders
had left him in less than a year, and he had
been a firm and healthy man from thence forward, till the time he wrote this treatise; this
was in his eightieth year, and he lived to give
a third and fourth edition of it; and, after having passed his hundredth year, died without
pain or agony, and like one who falls asleep."

"The sentiments of the illustrious Socrates,
as recorded by the amiable Xenophon," said Sir
Hubert, "may serve to guide our arguments
and opinions on this subject. 'Temperance,'
says he, 'is that virtue, which places both the
body and the mind in their full state of per-

fection, and qualifies a man both for the knowledge and the practice of his duty :—enables
him to govern his family with prudence, to
serve his country and his friends in the most ef-
fectual manner, and to defeat the malice of his
enemies. The very consciousness of thus con-
forming to the dictates of nature, and qualify-
ing ourselves to be useful members of society,
must afford us a pleasure, which can never be
felt by the stupid voluptuary; who is so engaged in the pursuit of imaginary gratifica-
tions, that he is never at liberty to perform a
commendable action. Intemperance, though
it may promise pleasure, can never bestow it;
for true pleasure is only in the gift of Temperance.' Thus far this wise and amiable
man. To show the danger of intemperance,
the Catholic legends tell us of some hermit,
to whom the devil gave the choice of three
crimes; two of them of the most atrocious
kind, and the other to be drunk. The poor
saint chose the last, as the least of the three;
but, when drunk, he committed the other
two."

"What an excellent and striking apologue!"
cried Edmund. "But I really think we shall
not have much to say in favour of our heroes;

for, after all, I do not see any great merit
in not being a glutton. I cannot help laughing, though, to find, that the ladies have not
been able to produce a single instance of a
temperate woman; which, I suppose, they
would have done, for the honour of the sex,
if any had been recorded."

" There was no need to do this," answered
Emily, with vivacity; " because women are
so temperate, that one could not be selected
for example, without doing injustice to the
rest; while the men are generally so intem-
perate, that those we have mentioned are only
exceptions to the general rule."

The party laughed at the quickness of
Emily's repartee; and George added, " I am
afraid, Emily, your remark is not perfectly
correct, at least with respect to the ancients."

" Oh! I am not defending the cause of the
ancients, you know," said the lively girl: " but
what, were the ladies of old accustomed to
get tipsy?"

" We may conclude so," replied George,
" from some curious laws that were made on
the subject at Athens; and at Rome, one of
their chief men beat his wife to death, because
he caught her drinking out of the wine barrel:
and Cato, the censor, is said to have introdu-

ced the custom of persons kissing ladies, when they met them, or paid them a visit, to discover by their breath, whether they had been tipling. But come, Charles, have you nothing in praise of Alexander's temperance?"

"No, I really am of Edmund's opinion; I should not think much better of myself, because I gave the best peach or nectarine in the garden to Emily or Jane. Besides, the temperance of Alexander does not seem to have been very deeply rooted; for he forgot all the lessons of Leonidas, and died in a debauch."

"I cannot consent to think so lightly of the merits of Cyrus," said George: "there appears to me to be something extremely fascinating in his manners and conduct at the court of his grandfather."

"But this impression," observed Sir Hubert, "is no doubt to be, in a great measure, attributed to the elegant pen of the simple and classic Xenophon, who, in pourtraying the character of Cyrus, meant to give a representation of a perfectly amiable and accomplished prince."

"But surely we may suppose, my dear Sir," rejoined George, "that Xenophon did not select the character of Cyrus for this

purpose, without good reason; and, however
he may have embellished the portrait, the
truth of the character is still preserved."

"I should not think the conduct of Agesilaus very singular," said Edmund, "in distributing the luxuries presented to him by
the Thasians among his slaves, because temperance was the virtue of all the Spartans,
and formed a principal part of their education. If I recollect rightly, to give them an
early abhorrence to wine, their mothers used
to offer them cups of it, in which were put
live snakes; and to impress them more
strongly with a disgust for drunkenness, at
certain times they intoxicated their slaves,
the poor Helots, and in that state exhibited
them to their children. But when Agesilaus
rejected these presents, the Lacedæmonians
were at war, and then the soldiers were allowed to indulge in every sort of luxury. So
I cannot but think, that, in this case, the
good king showed that his was a real love of
temperance; when, if he had indulged in
luxury, it would only have been following
the custom of his country."

"Very ably argued, Edmund, upon my
word," said Lady Arborfield; and you have

o

displayed more historical knowledge than I thought you were master of."

"Your story of Socrates, papa," said Emily, "diverts me exceedingly. I cannot help fancying I see him throwing away his pitcher of water; I suppose he took pretty good care not to break his pitcher, or else his terrible wife, Xantippe, might perhaps have broken his head."

"You are very merry to-night, Emily," said Edmund, laughing heartily with the rest at her strange idea; "but you should not joke upon the misfortunes of poor Socrates, especially as he bore them so patiently. His temperance seems to have been very great," continued he, "since it preserved him from the effects of the plague, by which so many suffered. But as to his throwing away the water, I think I am as great a philosopher, or greater than he; for you know that, in summer time, when I am warm, if I am ready to die with thirst, I always hold the glass of water some minutes in my hand before I taste a drop; and, I am sure, this is a great trial of patience indeed."

"This is a very good method," observed Lady Arborfield, "to prevent the ill effects that would arise from drinking perfectly cold

water, when you are violently heated. By
holding it in your hand the water becomes
warmer, while you grow proportionably
cooler; so that, by this means, almost an
equal temperature is produced between your
blood and the water."

"Temperance," said Jane, "was only one
among the many virtues which distinguished
the illustrious Sully; but, like all the rest, it
attended him in all situations, and on all
occasions. No temptations, no example,
could induce him to depart from it; and, if
a strict perseverance in the practice of any
virtue can give a claim to eminence, to this
the virtuous Sully is certainly entitled."

"Oh, you must not think of ranking him
above my hero!" said Emily. "Consider,
there is more merit in leaving off bad habits,
than in persevering in good ones."

"If the motive be a good one," replied
Jane. "But you say that Charles made
Alexander and Cæsar his models, and that it
was from the moment that he prepared for
war that he gave up his luxurious course of
life. This shows that it was not from a love
of the virtue itself, but because he found,
by the example of Cæsar and Alexander, that
it would be useful to him in executing the

plans he meditated. My uncle will correct me if I am wrong; but, I believe, that it was the intention of Charles to conquer and enslave the world; and that he was scarcely any thing else but a brave madman; and, indeed, it is supposed that his own soldiers killed him, convinced that neither their own country, nor any other in Europe, would remain tranquil or happy while he lived. While such were his motives, we must not give him credit for his actions, or the virtues which he may appear to possess."

"You have no reason, my dear Jane," said Sir Hubert, "to apprehend correction from me. I am rather at a loss to express sufficiently to you, the satisfaction which I feel in the truth and acuteness of your reflections. Poor Emily's hero will certainly not obtain the palm to-night; and, my lady will excuse me, if I say, that Lewis Cornaro seems rather to have acted from necessity than principle. He was, indeed, a fortunate instance of the benefits resulting from a temperate life; and at length, perhaps, became so attached to it, that he would not, even if he could have done it with safety, have returned again to luxury. The question seems to rest then between Cyrus and Sully, and I am inclined to adjudge it in favour of the latter; for, though it was inconsistent with the plan of Xenophon to mention it, we learn from other historians, that Cyrus himself, for political purposes, introduced, at length, every species of excess which could add magnificence to royalty, and sowed the first seeds of that luxury, which soon overspread and corrupted the whole Persian empire."

On Sunday evening our good friends at Holly Hall had very properly chosen religion for the subject of their conversation; and Sir Hubert prefaced his story with the few following remarks:

"I was happy to see you were not surprised at my proposing religion for the subject of our amusement. Nothing can be more injurious to the cause of religion, than to represent it as an enemy to mirth and cheerfulness. It is not its intention to extirpate the affections of the mind, but to regulate them.

"Religion is such a sense of God on the soul, and such a conviction of our obligations to him, and dependance upon him, as should engage us to make it our principal study to do always that which we think will be pleasing to him, and to avoid every thing which we think will offend him.

"We may confidently affirm, that reli-

gion is natural to man, even in the most unenlightened state; nations, that never were
favoured with the knowledge of it by revelation, have, nevertheless, a belief, that there is
a Being, who rewards good men and punishes
the wicked. That the greatest and wisest of
men, in all ages and countries, felt and ac-
knowledged the presiding influence of a Su-
preme Power, I hope we shall be able to
produce sufficient examples to show.

"Agesilaus, king of Sparta, was, on all
occasions, distinguished by his particular veneration for the gods. The noblest circumstance of his victory over the Athenians and
Bœotians, at Chœronea, was his sacrificing his
resentment to the honour of religion; for a
considerable number of the flying enemy having thrown themselves into the temple of
Minerva, and application being made to him,
to know in what manner they should be
treated, he gave strict orders that none of
them should be touched, though he then la-
boured under the anguish of several wounds
he had received in the action, and was visi-
bly exasperated at the opposition he had
met. But his veneration was not confined
to the temples of the Greeks. When he

made war upon the barbarians, he was equally careful not to profane the images of their
deities, nor offer the least violation to their
altars."

"I will," said Edmund, "relate an instance
of the singular interference of Providence,
which is recorded by Jane's favourite author,
Plutarch.

"The brave Timoleon, the glory of Corinth, was the most pious of men: nothing
boastful or vain-glorious disgraced his lips. On
the contrary, when he heard his praises re-
sounded from street to street, and from city
to city, he only replied, 'that he rendered his
most humble thanks to the gods, that, when
they had decreed to rescue his country from
the usurpation of tyrants, they condescended
to make him the happy instrument;' for he
was of opinion, that all human occurrences
are conducted by the influence of heaven.
He had in his house a private chapel, in
which he constantly paid his devotions to the
goddess who represented Providence. To reward his piety, he was wonderfully protected
by the deity, in several instances of his life,
but particularly in the following:

"Three persons had entered into a con-
spiracy to assassinate him, as he was offering
up his devotions in a public temple.   To execute their horrid plan, they took their several
stands, in the most convenient places for
their purpose, intending afterwards to conceal
themselves, by mixing in the crowd, which
stood about him; but, while they were watching for an opportunity, a stranger suddenly
fell upon one of them, and stabbed him to the
heart.   The other two conspirators, concluding from this, that their plot had been discovered, and measures taken to prevent the execution of it, instantly threw themselves at
Timoleon's feet, and confessed the whole af-
fair.   This stranger, upon examination, was
found to have known nothing of their design;
but having, several years before, had a brother
killed by the conspirator he had now dis-
pathed, and having long waited for an opportunity of revenge, he at last discovered him
in the temple, where he had planted himself
for the villanous purpose of depriving the
good Timoleon of life."   Plutarch concludes
his account of this transaction in a pious rapture on the watchful care of Providence;
which, in this instance, had so ordained it,
that the stranger should so many years be

debarred the means of doing justice to his
brother, till, by the same blow that revenged
the death of one innocent man, he preserved
the life of another.

"Though Plutarch is generally accused,"
remarked Sir Hubert, "of being weakly su-
perstitious, I do not think he can be thought
so in this instance; as the same reflection, I
should conceive, would naturally occur to every
pious mind."

"You have told me, Sir," said Charles,
"that I should not give credit to relations of
supernatural appearances; yet, as the circumstance, which, I confess, has made a great impression on my mind, is told of a very religious
man, by the great and good Cicero, I hope I
shall not offend you by relating it."

"When King Hiero asked Simonides, the
famous poet, what he thought of the Deity,
he requested a day to consider of it. When
that was expired, he requested two days
more; and still, as the question was repeated,
he demanded double the time. This evasion
exciting the king's curiosity, he, at length, desired to know the reason of it. 'Sire,' replied
the venerable bard, ' the subject is so incom-

prehensible, that the longer I consider it, the more I am lost!' In his poems, this pious man exerted all the powers of his genius, to celebrate the praises of the gods.

"Having agreed to compose a panegyric for a Grecian champion, who had lately won a prize, he wrote a poem, in which he introduced the praises of Castor and Pollux, two inferior deities, who had formerly distinguished themselves in the same kind of exercises. The champion, though he could not help commending the poem, paid him but one-third of the price which he had promised him; and, when the poet demanded the rest, he answered, ' You must apply to the two gods for their share, to whom you have given two-thirds of the praise that you ought to have given to to me: but, that you may not imagine that I resent your partiality, I insist upon your company to supper.' Though Simonides was sensible that he had been defrauded, he resolved rather to suppress his indignation, than give offence to his new patron. He, therefore, accepted his invitation. In the midst of the entertainment, two beautiful young men, of more than human form, appeared at the gate, and requested that Simonides might be informed, that two strangers requested to

see him immediately, on some particular business. The servant did as he was desired;
but Simonides had scarcely stepped out of the
dining-room, before the roof fell in, and buried
all the rest of the company under the ruins.
As no young men were afterwards found at
the gate, it was universally concluded, that
the two strangers were the deities, who had
been celebrated by the poet; and that they
had taken this method to reward his piety,
and recompense the loss, which he had sus-
tained by the injustice of the champion."

Sir Hubert smiled at the recollection of
what he had said to Charles, when he had
proposed to tell the story of a ghost, on the
first evening; but he forbore all comment for
the present, and George took up the subject
thus:

"When the Gauls, after making themselves masters of Rome, were besieging the
capitol, and taking every precaution to prevent a single citizen from escaping, a pious
young Roman attracted the universal admiration, both of his fellow-citizens and of the
enemy. It was the stated custom of the Fabii,
one of the most illustrious families in Rome,

to offer an annual sacrifice upon the Qui-
rinal hill. For this purpose, Caius Fabius
Dorso, which was the name of the young and
devout hero, descended from the capitol, with
the sacred utensils in his hands, marched
through the midst of the enemy, and reached
the hill in safety. After he had finished the sacrifice, he returned by the same road he went,
and with the same intrepidity in his air and
countenance, not doubting but the gods, whose
honour he had thus been celebrating, at the
hazard of his life, would be his guardians and
protectors. His hopes were not disappointed;
for he passed through the enemy's camp, and
rejoined his countrymen in the capitol, without having received the least injury; the
Gauls, it is supposed, being either stupified
with astonishment at such a prodigy of youthful valour, or disarmed by the force of religion."

"Indeed," said Edmund, "I think this
young Roman deserved a public triumph, on
this occasion, as much as any general amongst
them, as he certainly evinced greater courage
than it was possible they should, and his motive far excelled any that the best of them
could ever make pretence to."

P

"He assuredly deserved such a distinction, Edmund," said Sir Hubert, "but, as true piety is always accompanied by humility, I do not doubt but it would have been declined by the pious young hero. All these were heathens," continued he, "who had nothing but the light of natural religion to guide their piety; I should suppose it will not be difficult to find, among those who have had the advantage of revelation, a degree of devotion as much more exemplary as their object is more defined."

"It would certainly be easy," replied Lady Arborfield, "to produce a long list of persons who have been persecuted, and suffered the most excruciating tortures, and even death, for the sake of the Christian religion; but, as true devotion consists more in a regular performance of our duty, and a perfect resignation to the will of the Deity, than in violent sacrifices, I shall repeat what has been related of the virtuous Addison; which, though not rendered so interesting by its striking incident, as those anecdotes, with which you have favoured us, does him no less credit for his piety.

"This good man, after a long and manly,

but fruitless struggle with the distemper of which he died, dismissed his physicians, and with them all hopes of life. He dismissed not, however, his concern for the living; but sent for the young Lord Warwick, a youth, nearly related to him, and finely accomplished, yet not above being the better for good impressions from a dying friend. He came; but life was now glimmering in the socket, the dying friend was silent. After a decent and proper pause, the youth said, ' Dear Sir, you sent for me, I believe, and I hope you have some commands; be assured, I shall hold them most sacred.' May distant ages not only hear, but feel the reply! Forcibly grasping the young nobleman's hand, he softly said, ' See in what peace a Christian can die!' He spoke with difficulty, and soon after expired."

" That truly pious man, Dr. Young, whose words I quote on this occasion, concludes with these devout and just reflections: ' Through divine grace, how great is man! through divine mercy, how stingless is death!' who would not thus expire?"

" My story is equally simple," said Emily.

" M. du Fresne took occasion one day to
remark to Louis XIV. that he did not appear
to be sufficiently cautious in the liberty,
which he gave to every one to approach his
person; and more particularly when he was
at war with a people, the Dutch, who were
irritated against him, and were capable of attempting any thing. 'I have received, Sir,'
said Louis, 'a great many hints like this; in
short, if I were capable of taking them, my
life would not be worth having; it is in the
hands of God, he will dispose of it as he
pleases; and, therefore, I do not presume to
make the least alteration in my conduct.' "

" We must lament," said Sir Hubert,
" that this great monarch did not regulate all
his actions by such sentiments. If he had,
this advice of his friends had been unneces-
sary; for then so many people would not
have had just reason to wish his death. It
is indeed said, that, before he died, he was
himself convinced of the folly of his life, and
wished that he could live it over again, to
plant the olive of peace where he had spread
the flames of war."

" You will not, I believe, my dear uncle,"
said Jane, " be able to make the same objec-

tion to the king, of whom I mean to speak; for he fought for the liberty of his subjects, and not for the purpose of enslaving others."

" Gustavus Adolphus, of Sweden, united, with the virtues which adorned his character, the most exemplary piety. Among the many instances of which, it is related of him, that once, when he was in his camp before Werben, he had been alone in the cabinet of his pavilion for some hours; and, on these occasions, none of his attendants durst interrupt him. At length, however, a favourite of his, urged by some important business which he had to communicate to him, came softly to the door, and, looking in, he beheld the king, in the most devout attitude, at his prayers. Fearing to interrupt him in this sacred employment, he withdrew his head, and would have retired; but his royal master, who had seen him, bid him come in, saying, ' Thou wonderest to see me in this posture, since I have so many subjects to pray for me; but I tell thee, that no man has more need to pray for himself than he, who being to render an account of his actions to none but God, is, for that reason, more closely assaulted by the

devil than all other men beside.' He could
not bear to receive that homage which he
conceived due only to the Deity; for, when
the town of Landshut, in Bavaria, surrendered
to him at discretion, and the principal inhabitants fell on their knees, to present him the
keys of their town, 'Rise, rise,' said he; ' it is
your duty to fall upon your knees to God,
and not to so frail and feeble a mortal as
I am.' And as he would not receive, so
neither would he pay, earthly homage. In a
treaty between Louis XIII. of France, and
Gustavus, the ministers of the former were
desirous of insisting that the king of France
had the king of Sweden under his protection.
Gustavus replied: 'I have no occasion for
any protection but that of God, and I desire
no other. After God I acknowledge no superior; and I wish to owe the success of my
arms to my sword and my good conduct
alone.' It was one of the maxims of this
pious monarch, that a man made a better
soldier in proportion to his being a better
Christian."

"Gustavus was, indeed," said Sir Hubert,
"one of those superior mortals that appear,
once in an age, to show men of what perfec-

tion human nature is capable. He was a patriot king; the very soul of honour, as brave as pious, and as merciful as brave."

"Oh, my dear Sir!" said Edmund, "after this panegyric upon Gustavus, what expectation can we have of obtaining the victory for our heroes. I suppose we had better give up the contest at once."

"Oh no, by no means!" replied Sir Hubert; "and, in the first place, therefore, let us hear your comment on the conduct of Agesilaus."

"I do not perceive," said George, "but that Agesilaus had a perfect sense of religion, and did not forget it under any circumstances. Neither the prospect of advantage, nor revenge, could stifle it in his bosom; nor was he bigotted to one particular form of worship; for he treated the altars of barbarians with as much reverence as those of the gods he worshipped himself."

"What can I say for Timoleon," said Edmund, "more than is said by Plutarch. He speaks expressly of his piety, of his private chapel, where he performed his devotions constantly in secret; the greatest proof of his sincerity. And his piety was well known to his countrymen, since the assassins,

who sought to murder him, selected a place
of worship for their purpose, well knowing
that he would come there, and that his
thoughts would be so entirely engrossed by
the divinity, that he would be off his guard."

" You smiled, my dear Sir," said Charles,
" at my story of Simonides and his two gods.
I suppose you thought, as Simonides was a
poet, the whole was a poetical invention."

" I smiled, Charles, at the recollection of
your love for the marvellous. It is a very
pretty story, and well calculated to impress a
belief in Providence; but, as you imagine,
there is more of poetry, I suspect, than of truth
in it. The answer of Simonides, however, to
the king, on the nature of the divinity, shows
how justly he had reflected on the subject."

"Which ought I to praise most," said
George, " the pious intrepidity of young
Fabius, or the religious forbearance of the
Gauls? Which showed most reverence for
the Deity, he who dared to pass alone through
a band of enraged barbarians, or they, who
suffered him to pass,—they, who had sworn
the death of every other Roman?"

"Young Fabius, certainly," said Emily,
" is most to be admired, because it is certainly more admirable to do a noble action than

not to do a base one; and how base, and how
inhuman, would it have been in the Gauls,
if they had offered any violence to this brave
youth, when he was on so pious an errand."

"I thank you, Emily," replied George,
"for having so well expressed my own ideas
upon the subject. Fabius was the worthy son
of a house of heroes."

"The nature of my story does not admit
much of comment," said Lady Arborfield.
"The whole tenor of Addison's life was virtuous; this we know from others, but we
know it best from himself. His death bed
was illuminated by hope; and though the
most modest of men, he confidently expressed
his reliance on the mercy and goodness of his
God."

"Papa does not seem inclined," said
Emily, "to admit Louis XIV. among sincere
Christians; I am sure, therefore, I will not
presume to undertake his defence."

"You mistake me, Emily; I did not mean
to say, that Louis was not sincere at last.
It would be uncharitable to suppose that he
affected what he did not feel; but his whole
soul was engrossed by ambition, and it was
only when he had exhausted all the fuel
which supplied this passion, that he fled to

religion as a resource against the tediousness of a listless existence."

" You have praised Gustavus so liberally, my dear uncle," said Jane, " that any thing which I could add would only weaken the effect of what you have been kind enough to say."

" You do yourself injustice," replied the worthy baronet; " but we will not trouble you, as our minds are sufficiently impressed with the merits of the great Gustavus. And now, I must confess, that a task of considerable difficulty and delicacy devolves on me; and this is occasioned chiefly by the necessity of taking into consideration the different objects of devotion. Indeed, all comparison between the ancients and moderns, in this respect, is impossible, except on the broad ground of natural religion; for, if we take revelation into the question, we must exclude the ancients, or we shall judge them unfairly. On so serious a subject I would rather not come to any particular decision. If the ancients made good use of the light of natural religion, the moderns do not seem to have profited less by the brighter beams of Christianity."

―――――――

"As our company arrive to-morrow," said Sir Hubert, when the party were assembled on Monday evening, " and this is, consequently, the last night that we shall be able to pursue our present mode of amusement, it is not without reason that we have selected honour for our theme; for honour may be said to be the refinement of virtue. It is that polish, which gives lustre to all other good qualities; and a man cannot be said to be truly honourable, who is absolutely deficient in any virtue."

" The deputies of Philip, king of Macedon, offering great sums of money, in that prince's name, to Phocion, the Athenian, and entreating him to accept them, if not for himself, at least for his children, who were in such circumstances that it would be impossible for them to support the glory of his name, 'If they resemble me,' said Phocion, 'the little

spot of ground, on the produce of which I
have hitherto lived, and which has raised me
to the glory you mention, will be sufficient to
maintain them; if it will not, I do not intend
to have them wealthy merely to foment and
heighten their luxury.

"After this, Alexander the Great, the
son of Philip, having sent him a hundred talents, Phocion asked those who brought them,
upon what design Alexander had sent him so
great a sum, while he did not remit any to
the rest of the Athenians. 'It is,' replied
they, 'because Alexander looks upon you
as the most just and virtuous man.' Then
answered Phocion, 'let him suffer me still to
enjoy that character, and be really what I am
taken for.'"

"It is a pity," said George, "that he
could not inspire his countrymen with such
sentiments of honour, he would then have
spared them the reproach of being taught it
by one whom they styled a barbarian."

"Demetrius Poliorcetes, who had performed great services for the city of Athens,
on setting out for a war in which he was engaged, left his wife and children to the pro-

tection of the Athenians. His army was entirely defeated, and it was with great difficulty that he saved himself, by flight, from
falling into the hands of his enemies. He did
not doubt, however, but that he should find
a safe asylum among his good friends, the
Athenians; but those ungrateful men refused
to receive him, and even sent back to him his
wife and children, under pretence that they
might probably not be safe in Athens, where
the enemy might come and take them. This
conduct pierced the heart of Demetrius; for
nothing is so affecting to an honourable mind
as the ingratitude of those we love, and on
whom we have conferred obligations.

" Some time afterwards Demetrius reco-
vered his affairs, and came with a large army
to lay siege to Athens. The Athenians, per-
suaded that they had no pardon to expect
from Demetrius, determined to die sword in
hand; and passed a decree, which condemned
to death those who should first propose to
surrender to that prince; but they did not
recollect, that there was but little corn in the
city, and that they would, in a short time, be
in want of bread. Want soon made them
sensible of their error; and after having suffered hunger for a long time, they began to

Q

say, ' It would be better that Demetrius
should kill us at once, than for us to die by
the lingering torments of famine; perhaps he
will have pity on our wives and children.'
They then opened to him the gates of the
city.

" Demetrius, having taken possession of
the city, ordered that all the married men
should assemble in a spacious place appointed
for the purpose; and that the soldiery, sword
in hand, should surround them. Cries and
lamentations were then heard from every
quarter of the city; women embracing their
husbands, children their parents, and all taking an eternal farewell of each other.

" When the married men were all thus
collected, Demetrius, from an elevated situation, reproached them for their ingratitude
in such a feeling manner and pathetic terms,
that he himself could not help shedding tears.
He then, for some time, remained silent;
while the Athenians expected that the next
word he uttered would be, to order his soldiers
to massacre them all.

" It is hardly possible to imagine their
surprise, when they heard that good prince
say, ' I wish to convince you how ungene-
rously you have treated me; for it was not to

an enemy you refused assistance, but to a prince who loved you, who still loves you, and who wishes to revenge himself only by granting your pardon, and by being still your friend. Return to your own homes: while you have been here, my soldiers have been filling your houses with provisions!"

"To those who had any feeling," said Edmund, "this kindness of Demetrius must have been almost worse than death."

"I am afraid they could not feel it as they ought," replied Emily; "or they would not have behaved so ungratefully at first."

"I believe you are right, Emily," observed Lady Arborfield; for ingratitude, when it has once taken possession of the heart, excludes every generous sentiment, and engrosses it entirely."

"There is a very pretty story," said Edmund, "which I read lately in Cæsar's Commentaries. It is a curious sort of challenge, and shows how differently the Romans settled their honourable disputes to what we do now-a-days."

"Two centurions, of high rank, Titus Pulfio and Lucius Varenus, had long disputed,

with great animosity, which was the braver
man, or most worthy of preferment. They
served under Cæsar in Gaul; and once, when
his camp was assaulted by the enemy, in the
heat of the attack, Pulfio cried aloud, 'Why
should you remain in doubt, Varenus? What
better opportunity can you desire to prove
your boasted valour? This, this shall be the
day to decide our controversies.' He then immediately sallied from the camp, and rushed
upon the enemy. Varenus followed his rival,
who, with his javelin, had already slain the
first of the Gauls that engaged him; but
being attacked by a shower of darts, one of
them pierced his shield, and stuck in his belt
in such a manner as prevented him from
drawing his sword. The enemy immediately
surrounded him, thus encumbered and unable to defend himself. At this instant, when
he must have fallen beneath their swords,
Varenus, perceiving his danger, flew to his
assistance, slew one, and drove the rest before
him; but, pursuing them too eagerly, he stepped into a hole, and fell down. Pulfio, who
had now disencumbered himself from the
dart, and drawn his sword, came very season-
ably to the rescue of Varenus; with whom,
after having slain many of the Gauls, he re-

turned with safety and glory to the camp,
and they continued friends ever afterwards."

"Their friendship could not fail to be
permanent," said Sir Hubert, "formed on so
honourable a basis. Friendship cannot exist
unsupported by honour. No confidence can
be placed in a man destitute of this principle;
and hence it is, that the wicked, in their iniqui-
tous leagues, are in constant dread of being
betrayed by each other."

"Many examples of honourable conduct,"
said Charles, "are to be found in the history
of the Romans, so that one is almost at a loss
which to select. Indeed it has been observed,
that the reputation of the Romans for equity,
humanity, clemency, and constancy to their engagements, contributed more than any thing
besides to make their empire so extensive and
powerful. But, with the following instance
of honour and justice, I have always been
particularly pleased."

"The Falisci, a Grecian colony, settled
in Italy, had attacked the Romans without
provocation, who instantly denounced war
against them, and intrusted the conduct of it
to their dictator, Camillus. He immediately

besieged their principal city, surrounding it
with trenches, so as to cut off all communication with the country; but leaving a considerable space between them and the walls.
It seems the Falisci had brought with them
from Greece the custom of intrusting the education of all their children to the care of one
man, called the pedagogue The children were
accustomed to walk with their master without
the walls of the city; and, as the Roman
camp was at a considerable distance, it was
not thought necessary to discontinue their
exercise.   But the present pedagogue proved
a traitor.   He at first led his pupils only
along the walls; then he carried them a little
farther; and, at length, when a favourable
opportunity offered, he led them through the
guards of the Roman camp quite to the general's tent.   As they were the children of the
best families in the place, their treacherous
leader, when he came into Camillus's presence, addressed him thus: 'With these
children I deliver the place you besiege into
your hands; they were committed to my care
and tuition; but I prefer the friendship of
Rome to my employment at Falerii.'   Camillus was struck with horror at the treachery; and
looking at him with a menacing air, 'Traitor!'

said he, 'you do not address yourself, with
your impious present, either to a general or a
people that resemble you. We have, indeed,
no express and formal alliance with the Falisci; but that which nature has established
between all men, does, and shall subsist between us. War has its rights as well as
peace; and we have learned to make it with
no less justice than valour. We are in arms,
not against an age which is spared even in
cities taken by assault, but against men armed
like ourselves; men who, without any pre-
vious injury from us, attacked the Roman
camp at Veii. Thou, to the utmost of thy
power, hast imitated them by a new and different sort of crime; but, for me, I shall conquer, as at Veii, by Roman arts, by valour,
works, and perseverance.'

"The traitor was not dismissed with this
reprimand only; Camillus caused him to be
stripped, and to have his hands tied behind
him; and, arming the young scholars with
rods, he ordered them to drive him back into
the city, and to scourge him all the way;
which no doubt they did with a good will.

"At this sight the Falisci, who had been
inconsolable for the loss of their children,
raised cries of joy; they were charmed to such

a degree, with so uncommon an example of justice and honour, that, in an instant, they entirely changed their disposition in respect to the Romans, and resolved that moment to have a peace with such generous enemies. Accordingly they sent deputies, first to the camp, and afterwards to Rome; where, when they had audience of the senate, they addressed themselves to it in these terms: ' Illustrious fathers, conquered by you and your general, in a manner that can give no offence to gods or men, we are come to surrender ourselves to you; and we assure ourselves, than which nothing can be more glorious for victors, that we shall live happier under your government than under our own laws. The event of this war has brought forth two excellent examples for mankind. You, fathers, have preferred justice to immediate conquest; and we, excited by that justice and honour which we admire, voluntarily present you the victory."

" Where could this contemptible pedagogue," said Emily, " hide his shame? for I suppose the Falisci despised him too much to put him to death."

"I do not recollect," replied Charles, " whether it is mentioned how he was punished; though, I think, the greatest punishment that could be inflicted on him, would be to suffer him to live; for, where could he hide himself from scorn; or whither could he fly from detestation and contempt?"

"The story you have told us," said Lady Arborfield, "proves the truth of the observation, with which you introduced it. I do not doubt, however, to convince you, that the sense of honour has not declined in modern times; and the Spaniards are particularly distinguished for it."

"In the year 1746, when, as you recollect, we were at war with Spain, a merchant ship of London, richly laden, coming through the Gulf from Jamaica, encountered a most violent storm; and, springing a leak, was forced to run into the Havannah, a Spanish port, to save the lives of the crew. The captain went on shore, and immediately waited on the governor; and telling him the occasion, that had forced him to seek shelter in the port, offered to surrender the ship as a prize, and himself and men as prisoners of war, requesting only good treatment. 'No, Sir,' replied the Spanish governor: 'if we had taken you in fair war, at sea, or approaching our coast with hostile in-

tentions, your ship would then have been a
prize, and your people prisoners; but when,
distressed by a tempest, you come into our
ports for the safety of your lives, though we
are your enemies, we are men, and as such,
are bound by the laws of humanity, to afford
relief to distressed men, who ask it of us.
We cannot, even against our enemies, take
advantage of an act of God. You have leave,
therefore, to unload your ship, if that be necessary, to stop the leak; you may refit her
here, and traffic so far as shall be necessary to
pay the charges; you may then depart, and I
will give you a pass, to be in force till you are
beyond Bermuda; if, after that, you are taken,
you will then be a lawful prize; but now, you
are only a stranger, and have a stranger's
right to safety and protection.' The ship,
after repairing her damages, accordingly, departed, and arrved safe in the Thames."

"This honourable spirit," said Emily,
"which so much distinguishes the Spaniards,
was brought into Spain, I have read, by the
Moors, and I remember a very interesting
story on the subject.

"A Spanish cavalier, in a sudden quarrel,

slew a Moorish gentleman, and fled. His pursuers soon lost sight of him, for he had, un-
perceived by them, leapt over a garden wall.
The owner, a Moor, happened to be walking
in his garden; and the Spaniard, falling on his
knees, acquainted him with his situation, and
implored concealment. ' Eat this,' said the
Moor, giving him half a peach; 'you now
know that you may confide in my protection.'
He then locked him up in a summer-house,
in the garden, promising, as soon as it was
night, to provide for his escape to a place of
greater security. The Moor then went into
the house, where he had scarcely seated himself, when a great crowd, with loud lamentations, came to his gate, bearing the corpse of
his son, who had just been killed, they said,
by a Spaniard.

" When the first shock of surprise was a
little over, he learnt, from the description
given, that the fatal deed was done by the
very person then in his power. He mentioned this to no one; but, as soon as it was dark,
retired to his garden, as if to mourn alone;
giving orders that none should follow him.
Then, accosting the Spaniard, he said, ' Christian, the person you have killed is my son :
his bleeding body now lies in my house. You

ought to suffer; but, you have eaten with me,
and I have given you my faith, which must
not be broken.' He then led the astonished
Spaniard to his stables, and mounting him on
the fleetest horse he had, 'Fly far,' said he,
' while the night can cover you; by day-light
you will be beyond the reach of danger. Your
hands, indeed, are steeped in the blood of my
son, but God is just and good, and I thank
him that I am innocent of yours; and, that
the faith I gave, I have had sufficient courage
to preserve."

" What did the Moorish gentleman mean,
by giving half the peach, and telling the
Spaniard he had eaten with him, and, therefore, saved him?" enquired Edmund.

" It is an Eastern custom," replied Lady
Arborfield, " which you often find alluded to
in the Holy Scriptures; and, which is preserved,
in those countries, even to this day. Hospitality is the virtue of the East, and a very necessary one, where there are no inns, as in Europe,
and the villages lie at a great distance asun-
der. The traveller is sure to find welcome in
every house, even in the tents of the wandering
and predatory Arabs. Eating together is considered the symbol and pledge of friendship;

and, after this ceremony, persons, who never
met before, are ready to sacrifice themselves
in the defence of the person or property of
each other. That man, who should betray
the rights of hospitality, would be rejected
from their society, as something too vile to
associate with him."

"The sentiment of honour," said Jane,
"does not appear to be confined either to one
age, or to one quarter of the globe. We meet
with a remarkable instance of it, in the conduct of a poor unenlightened African.

"A New-England sloop, on a trading voyage to Guinea, in 1752, left their second mate,
William Murray, sick on shore; and, not being
able to wait for his recovery, sailed without
him. Murray was entertained at the hut of
a negro, named Cudjoe, with whom he had
made an acquaintance during their trade. As
the ship was gone, Murray, after the sickness
had left him, was still obliged to continue
with his black friend, till some other opportunity should offer for his return home. In
the mean time, a Dutch vessel came into the
road, and some of the negroes, going on board,
were treacherously seized, and carried off as
slaves. The relations and friends, transport-

ed with sudden rage, flew instantly to the house of Cudjoe, to wreak their vengeance upon poor Murray; but Cudjoe stopped them at the door, and demanded what they wanted. 'The white men,' said they, 'have carried off our brothers and our sons, and we will kill all white men. Give us the white man in your house, for we will kill him.'—'Nay,' said Cudjoe, 'the white men, that carried off your relations, are bad men, kill them when you can take them; but this white man is a good man, and you must not kill him.'—'But he is a white man,' they cried, 'and the white men are all bad men; we will kill them all.'—'No, my friends,' said he, 'you must not kill a man who has done you no harm, merely because he is white. This man is my friend, my house is his castle, I am his soldier, and must fight for him. You must kill me before you shall kill him. What good man will ever come under my roof again, if I let my floor be stained with a good man's blood?'—The negroes seeing his resolution, and being convinced, by what he said, that they were wrong, went away ashamed. A few days afterwards, Murray ventured abroad again with his friend Cudjoe, when several of the negroes took him kindly by the hand, and told him, they were very

glad they had not killed him; for, as he was
a good man, their God would have been very
angry, and would have spoiled their fishing."

"What a charming fellow!" cried Edmund; "I fancy I see his honest black face
at the door of his hut, expressing all the courage of his soul."

"What a situation for Murray!" added
Emily, "to see his friendly host on the point
of being sacrificed for him. But we must
now begin our argument."

"The first story that was told," said
George, "was that of Phocion refusing the
presents of Philip, and of his son Alexander.
We know that Phocion's whole life was a life
of honour. He had a just idea of the value
of money; and his means, though small, were
greater than his wants. He did not seek for
profitable employments in the state; it would,
therefore, have been very inconsistent with
the whole character of his life, if he had
stooped to accept of presents from a prince,
whose power, he well knew, was dangerous
to the safety of his country, and whose ambition surpassed his power. Presents from such
a man he could not but consider as bribes;
he might well, therefore, disdain them, for

they would have disgraced a man much less
distinguished than the illustrious Phocion."

"So then," said Sir Hubert," you allow
Phocion, in this instance, " only negative merits; I believe you are pretty right."

" Taking only into consideration," resumed George, " the two incidents, as they
have been related to-night, we cannot, I
think, do otherwise than feel a much higher
degree of admiration of the conduct of Demetrius. He had conferred benefits on the
Athenians, and thought himself so sure of
their attachment, that he trusted to their care
what was dearest to him in the world, his
wife and children. When he was unfortunate, and, as they thought, no longer able to
serve them, they not only refused him all
assistance, but even a shelter to his wife and
children. How honourable then was his conduct! when their fate was in his hands; when,
by a word, he could have annihilated them,
forgetful of the injuries and insults they had
heaped upon him, he gave them a noble instance of a monarch's vengeance; he spared
their lives, and fed their starving children, and
only asked their friendship in return."

"The conduct of the two centurions," said
Edmund, "did honour to them both; but

there is a great difference between them. Varenus, who sacrificed all animosity the moment he perceived his rival in danger, and
instantly fled to his rescue, is certainly entitled to a higher degree of praise than Pulfio,
who merely followed the example of Varenus,
and extricated him from a danger in which
he had been involved by his generous intrepidity."

"Your distinction is just, Edmund," said
Sir Hubert; "this was a race of honour, in
which Varenus nobly led the way."

"I am afraid," said Charles, "I am not
sufficiently impressed with the merits of the
Roman dictator, and I may, therefore, do him
injustice. I admire his conduct when I consider it alone; but, when I compare it with
that of Demetrius, as George has painted it, I
own I think it less extraordinary. The mind
of Camillus was too noble to owe success to
treason; and we see the dignity of his soul in
his address and conduct to the traitor. But
he had no resentments to sacrifice, as Demetrius had; and, had he taken advantage of
the traitor's offer, he would have shared his
infamy. While Demetrius, had he sacrificed
the Athenians to his wrongs, would only

R 3

have been considered to have executed an act of just retaliation."

"This is very liberal, indeed," said George; "and, I confess, more than I had a right to expect."

"As I do not think," said Lady Arborfield, "that we shall be able to rival Demetrius, we must make him the standard by which to judge of the merits of the rest. For instance, the Spanish governor gave up, to his nice sentiments of honour, what would have been advantageous to his country as well as to himself. Even his enemies would have thought him justified in taking what fortune had thrown in his way. So far we may consider him as superior to Camillus; but the crew of this ship had never personally injured him, nor returned his kindnesses with ingratitude; and so far, therefore, the action is inferior to that of Demetrius."

"If I may venture to differ from you, mamma," said Emily, "I should think we may fairly compare the Moorish gentleman with Demetrius; for, you know the Spaniard had slain his son, and he not only did not punish him, when he was in his power, but even assisted him to escape the justice of his country."

"I am sure," said Jane, "that honest
Cudjoe will not sink in your opinion, because
the trial of his honour was not so severe as
that of Demetrius, or the Moorish gentleman;
for, the noble manner in which he defended
his guest and the rights of hospitality, shows
that the true spirit of honour was deeply
rooted in his nature."

"We now then come to a conclusion,"
said Sir Hubert; "and it is certainly between
Demetrius and the Moorish gentleman that we
have to decide. I am not aware that any thing
can be added to what George has said, in il-
lustration of the merits of Demetrius; but
those of the Moorish gentleman must be further explained. We must recollect the mutual national antipathy of the Spaniards and
the Moors; and the abhorrence in which the
religion of the Moors taught them to hold a
Christian. The Spaniard seems to have been
aware of this, when, on finding the Moorish
gentleman in the garden, he fell on his knees
to him: for this was not an attitude in which
a high-spirited Spanish cavalier, as this gentleman appears to have been, would have
addressed another Spaniard on the same occasion. The Moorish gentleman at once displayed the native honour of his soul, when

he immediately granted protection to the enemy of his country and of his faith, who even confessed himself to have slain, that instant, one of his countrymen. The noble Moor gave him the peach to eat with him, to satisfy him that he was sincere; and having given this promise, honour so far conquered all other feelings, that his natural enemy, the murderer of his son, the man who had destroyed his hopes and plunged him in sorrow, received, at his hands, all the assistance that he could have expected from a generous friend. Demetrius had received his injuries from a whole people; his resentment was divided among a number of objects, and was, therefore, proportionably weakened. The Moor had received all his injuries from one, and his resentment was confined to him alone. Had Demetrius taken vengeance of the Athenians, and sacrificed them to his wrongs, many innocent victims must have perished; but the guilt of the Spaniard was certain, and, in destroying him, no injustice would have been committed. For these reasons I decide in favour of the Moor.

"And now, my dear children, good night. This is the last evening we shall be able to pass in this manner, for the present. I hope we are something wiser and better than when we began; and, as you seem to like this mode of diverting our time, we may resume our amusement when we meet again in the Easter holidays.   Good night!"

THE END.

Printed by J. Swan, 76, Fleet Street.

Printed in the United States
207273BV00003B/177/A